ABIRIBA
DICTIONARY
ABIRIBA-ENGLISH ENGLISH-ABIRIBA

Emeaba Onuma Emeaba

Emeaba

ABIRIBA DICTIONARY

ABIRIBA-ENGLISH ENGLISH-ABIRIBA

Published by Altrubooks Publishers
Houston, Texas.

Altrubooks First Edition, 2014

Printed in the United States of America

Library of Congress Cataloging-in-Publication Data is available on file

EMEABA EMEABA

ABIRIBA DICTIONARY
ABIRIBA-ENGLISH ENGLISH-ABIRIBA

Altrubooks Publishers
Houston, Texas

Emeaba

Dedicated to the memory of my father
Chief Onuma Kalu Emeaba (*Ete-Ikpa*)

Acknowledgements

I want to thank Professor Jean Casagrande, the head of department of Linguistics at the University of Florida where I started doing my research doctorate in Linguistics. We got talking one day. He was not only fascinated by my first name being the same as my last name, but also wanted to know why our culture should embrace such a naming system where the first son is named after his grandfather. In that conversation, he was made to understand that Abiriba language had never been written. Then, he said something very profound to me: "Why don't you write it?"

So, here is to you, professor.

Other people have contributed to this book. I particulary thank my wife, Ijeagu-*the gift*, for being the sounding board.

I thank others who have helped in one way or the other to see to the completion of this book. However, all imperfections in this book are mine.

Emeaba

Foreword

As part of the Igbo language, the Abiriba-Igbo is unique. It is unique because, although we are located at the heart of Igboland, our forebears got here by the circuitous route of the Yakur tribe in the lower Sahara, to the Ekoi of the Upper Cross River, then on to Ena, Usukpam, Arochukwu, Udara-Ebuo (in present-day Ohafia clan), and from there to the present site of the Abiriba Kingdom. In all that movement, over tens of generations, the Abiriba version of the Igbo language has been infected with the nuances of language and thing/place names of the peoples and places we passed through. Thus do we have such item names (item names that are unique in Igboland) as *"okpokoro"* (for table), *"ekpem"* (for bottle), *"oterikang"* (for hurricane lamp), *"usan"* (for dish plate or bowl), *"ukom"* (for plantain), *"anaghukwa"* (for bicycle), etc.

It is not easy writing about a language—any language—without a point of reference. The book you have in your hand now is about words. True, words enable us to communicate, but only when we have a common understanding of what they mean. For lack of the said point of reference, the author of this book has relied heavily on his linguistic background. He has therefore earned our applause and deep gratitude for this seminal work on the Abiriba-Igbo language.

In modern times, Abiriba people have been not merely tourist-type travelers, but long-term sojourners. Arochukwu, Ozuakoli, Nkpa, Itu, Efianyong, Calabar and Fernando Po (Panya) were places the Abiriba people sojourned. Then we moved on to far places like Lagos, Cameroons, Togo, and now England, USA and the Far East. At the end of it all, Abiriba people will come home to Abiriba. But as we have travelled farther afield, Abiriba children are being born in these far-off lands, and even the grown-ups who do not have regular opportunity to use the language tend to forget some Abiriba words. Hence Dr. Emeaba Onuma Emeaba's work is important in more ways than one: children get to learn the language of their forebears, while adults refresh their knowledge of Abiriba words and idiomatic expressions. Even non-Abiriba members of the Igbo race acquire a better understanding of the Abiriba person's words and idioms.

It has been said that languages and their usage grow and change over time. So Emeaba's effort here is just the beginning. But it is a good beginning. Therefore, to all who read this foreword and the Abiriba-English dictionary that follows, I wish you clarity—of thought, of words, and of understanding.

Eze Kalu Kalu Ogbu IV
Enachioken of Abiriba,
Abia State of Nigeria.

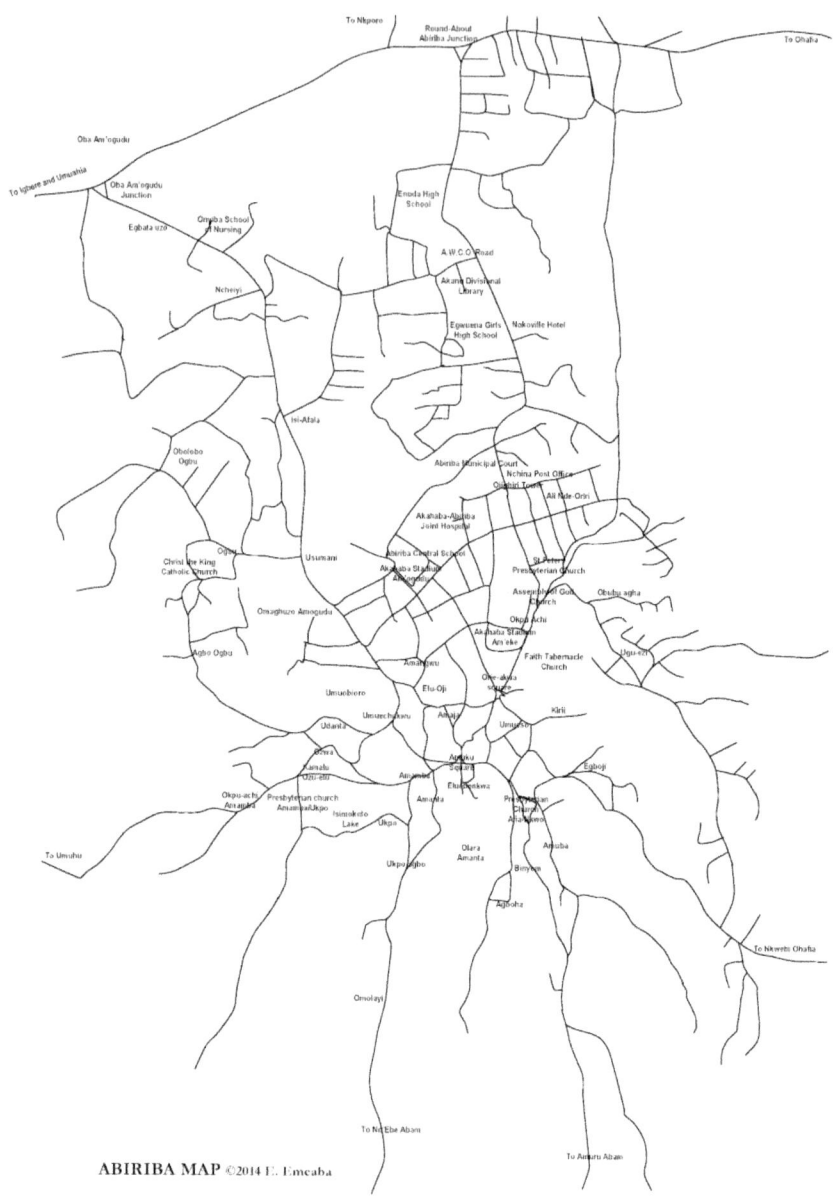

ABIRIBA MAP ©2014 E. Emeaba

Introduction

Preliminaries

To toot my own horn, I am a linguist with knowledge of the repertoire of six languages, and with a native-speaker proficiency in three. Abiriba language is one of the three. I have always loved languages and the study of languages. I have always believed that the knowledge of a people's language arms you with the knowledge of the people's way of life.

Unfortunately, with then colonialism, and now globalization, some of us are abandoning our mother tongues in a pitifully embarrassing way. Today, some languages are at various stages of endangerment. Children are now forced to speak English which will eventually result in no child speakers of the mother tongue available to continue where we left off. Soon, the number of users of the mother tongue gets smaller such that people begin to forget; and the language ultimately disappears.

Abiriba language has never been written, and there is almost no usable material on Abiriba reflecting any adequate analysis of the language. During my research studies at the University of Florida, I did some work on the language which forced the need for me to attempt the writing of this dictionary. In this first comprehensive and authoritative dictionary of Abiriba, I have collected meaningful discrete Abiriba free-forms and provided their meanings in English in as approximate a sense as I could. The book also includes an English-Abiriba index listing Abiriba equivalents for some English words.

There was a concerted effort in the gathering of information for this work. It must be noted, however, that I could not claim to have covered all the grounds in this project. This is basically an introduction to an Abiriba world view that deserves further attention. To that effect, I offer this, not as a last-word volume, but as a tool which both native and non-native users of Abiriba language will find useful.

This dictionary is written not only for you to use as a regular dictionary in looking up appropriate Abiriba words that correspond to an English word, but for you to browse through without any specific purpose, as if you were in a library of basic words.

Appeal

I believe there are quite a few Abiriba entry words that are missing here. I do not pretend to have mastered every detail of the language. If I continue to wait until I have all there is in Abiriba language, the publication of this book will continue to be delayed. I shall be glad if readers will note down any variations they find, any new grammatical forms, any missing entries, and any new words, and communicate them to me, so that later it may be possible to compile a more complete work. I appeal to readers to send those words, with their meanings, to altrubooks@gmail.com so that they would be included in the revised edition.

Background of the language

Abiriba (Ébíríbá) is part of a cluster of related languages commonly called Igbo—one of the three major ethnic and principal language groups of Nigeria—which share the same Niger-Congo *Bantu* roots with, and is structurally similar to, many other languages. The nature of the varieties of dialects in Igbo is such that some words commonly used in one area are not recognizable at all in another area. Verbal constructions and pronunciations in one area are completely different in other dialects. Some Igbo dialects are similar to a point of mutual intelligibility, but Abiriba language can sometimes stump other Igbo speakers to a point where Abiriba, spoken by over two hundred thousand people, has been described as a distinct language separate from Igbo.

Like most African languages, Abiriba is tonal. No prior linguistic study has been done on Abiriba, and its literature remains essentially oral.

There has been almost no usable material on Abiriba reflecting any adequate analysis of the language. The materials in the following dictionary are largely the product of an attempt by a native speaker linguist to capture the repertoire of a language that has never been written.

Some General Linguistic Features:
1. There are nine vowel phonemes: a e ɛ i ị o ɔ u ụ
   a. There is a vowel length, but it is of secondary importance here.
   b. Nasalized vowels are very common.
   c. Vowel assimilation is very regular to the extent that there is a tendency to vowel harmony.
2. In Abiriba, as well as in several other African languages, the co-articulated stops /gb/ and kp/ are realized as single unit implosives.
3. Abiriba has three distinctive tones.

Tones:

Tones are marked in Abiriba.

high: (marked with /′/)	lú	'be bitter'
	lá	'leak'
mid: (no marking)	lu	'told (a folktale)'
	la	'to go home'
low: (marked with /ˋ/)	lù	'make a mistake'
	là	'shave off (hair)'

Phonemes:

The alphabet for writing Abiriba is generally written thus:
a b ch d e ɛ f g ɡb gh gw ħ ħ̃ h i ị j k kp kw l m'm m̃ n ñ̃ ŋ nw ny o ɔ p r s sh t u ụ v w y z

Pronunciation
Consonants

Spelling	Description	Examples	
b, ch, d, g, v, f, m, n.	These consonants are pronounced the same as the corresponding sounds in English	bvá ɛbâ chɔ́ dèbé gáñé vúừ-vúừ fípừ míni námà	"Come here" "Want" "Keep" "Pass" "Being blown this way and that" "Edge out" "Water" "Cow"
k, p, t	These are similar to the corresponding English consonants	kálá pápừ từpwó	"Look at" "Carry away" "Open (a door, book, etc)"
gb, kp	These are technically labio-velar stops, voiced and voiceless respectively, and are pronounced with simultaneous closure at the lips (/b/ or /p/) and at the soft palate (/g/ or /k/)	gbàtú kpàyí	"Write down" "Speak; Talk"
gh	Similar to the *gh* in the English *aghast*	ghàyí	"Lie"
gw	Similar to the English *Gwen*	gwòsá	"Bring"
kw	Pronounced as *q* in *quarter*, it is a voiceless labialized velar plosive.	Kwà-mádũ	"Each person"
'm	Pronounced as the *m* in *combine*	ḿbè	"Tortoise"

m̃	The closest English equivalent is the *cm* sound in *acme*.	m̃àfé	"Jump over"
s, z	These are similar to the corresponding sounds in English	s̃hìé zɔ̀ɔ́	"Smell" "Step on"
ħ̆	In producing /ħ̆/, the air passes through a narrow passage formed by raising the back of the tongue towards the soft palate. This is technically a voiceless velar fricative	ħ̆ɔ̀rú	"Pick out; Choose for self"
ħ	This is similar to /ħ̆/ but produced somewhat further back in the mouth with nasalization. This is a voiced pharyngeal fricative with nasalization.	ħàtá	"Be equal"
ny	This is similar to the /ny/ in Sonya. It is a palatal nasal.	nyànɗé	"Adhere to"
ŋ	This is a velar nasal similar to the English sound *ng* in *sing*.	ŋ́chà	"Soap"
ŋ̃	Pronounced as the *ng* in *singer*	ŋ̃àbúkɔ́	Keel over"
j	Pronounced as in the English *joy*.	jùħú	"Be cool"

l	This is similar to the *l* in *letter* with a raised, flat tongue	làh̃é	"Go home"
r	A voiced alveolar fricative produced by letting air pass through a narrow passage formed by raising the tip of the tongue towards the ridge behind the upper teeth.	ré	"sell"
sh̃	Similar to the corresponding */sh/* sound in English *shin*	sh̃i	"Smell"
w, y	These are semi vowels similar to the corresponding sounds in English.	wá yé	"them" "add"

Vowels

Spelling	Description	Examples	
i	This is a high front unrounded vowel similar to the vowel in English *heat*	ìshì ímí	"blindness" "nose"
ị́	This is similar to the English vowel */i/* in *lit*	ị́pa	"to lift"
e	This is a centralized mid front unrounded vowel in the English *gate*.	éwú	"goat"

ɛ	This is a lower mid front unrounded vowel similar to the English *air*.	érá	"Madness"
a	This is a low central unrounded vowel similar to the English vowel in *arrow*.	átáŋ	"Bell"
ɔ	This is a lower mid back rounded vowel similar to the beginning vowel in the English *oral*.	ɔ́rú	"Fault"
u	This is a high back rounded vowel similar to the vowel in English *boot*.	úbì	"Farm"
ʮ	This pronounced as in *u* in English *fuller*	ʮ́tá	'Bow'

All of the above vowels have nasalized counterparts.

Emeaba

Part 1
Abiriba-English

a

a First letter of the alphabet.

à This, as in: īfêà (*this thing*).

á At, In, as in: Á'fyá *(at the market)*.

aà, aā Used as an exclamation.

ãá Yes (Answer to a call).

àbà Name of a tree and its fruits - a velvety black pod containing a seed covered in a succulent pollen-like substance.

Àbá A large town in Abia State of Nigeria that has the largest number of Ébịrịbá sojourners.

Àbàá A male name. People named Àbàá are also called Ŋḱúŋgw̃ù.

ábácħá White (cloth), sheet, or calico.

ábàchí Climbing plant producing large black hard-shelled seeds in a hairy pod. The seed when ground is used in food preparation as a thickener.

ábàchí Gizzard.

àbàdá Cloth. Wax printed cloth

àbàdábà Width. Broad; wide.

áɓàghị None fitting.

ábàghị-úrù Useless.

àbàlàkà An aggressive bird known to use other birds' feather for its nest.

àbàlì Night.

àbàlìdìmégw̃ù Armed robbers: Night marauders.

àbàlísì Dark of night.

Ábàm See Éɓàm.

ábáŋ Barrel made with wooden staves held together with metal bands or hoops. (Efik borrowing).

Àbánkpùghùrù The junction also called Round-About where the Ébịrịbá road meets with Ɔħàfya and Ŋkpóró roads.

àbáráwóm Flood. Excess flood water from an overflown river.

ábárìtághá A kind of beans with large seeds.

àbí A variety of yam, usually light yellow in color.

ábígbí Alphabet

Ábíríbá See Ébịrịbá.

àbịrịkɔ A kind of lizard that looks like a wall-gecko.

Ábú See **Ébyábu.**

áɓu Animal of the cat family said to be attracted to wine. A drunk.

ábùK̃é Small size. Never grows large, as in Ɔkúkù ábùK̃é: (*small sized fowl used mostly for sacrifices*).

ábwɔ́ Farm basket.

ábwɔ́-éK̃á Long rectangular farm basket made of bamboo.

ábwɔsí Species of tree (wood among those used to make tooth cleaning stick and the leaves burned for scent). Male name.

ábỹà (Rigorous) dance.

ábyaghị Failure to come; did not come.

ábyaghị-abya Absent; not come at all.

ábyaghị-ŋ́gw̃áŋgw̃à Late; not come on time.

ábyàmkpɔ́ Masquerade that dances on stilts.

áchankori (Of a girl) wild and boisterous.

áchí (1) A large tree producing flat, black seeds in a pod. The seeds dispersed by an explosive mechanism. In its ground form, áchí is used as a soup thickener. (2) ___Used as slang for___: Money.

àɗá First daughter. Female name, mostly first daughters.

áda See **ádàntá-ɔ̀kpú-ŋsK̃i.**

àdáka An arboreal anthropoid ape, having large ears and dark brown hair, and smaller and more intelligent than the gorilla.

ádám Paddle. Oars.

ádantà-ɔkpú-ńsK̃í Dung beetle.

ádèmé It is a common practice.

àdígbòlója Fake. Artificial.

ádìghì Is not, ___as in___: Íshí ényí **ádìghì** ányì ényí ígbíjí (*the elephant's head is not heavy for the elephant*).

ádịya Less.

áfà Year.

áfàá This year.

àfáK̃i Past year, ___as in___: àfáK̃'ètɔ̀ (three years past.)

àfárà Sail (Efik borrowing).

áfàráǹcK̃ì A kind of split pod from a flowering plant used by children to stick between the ears in a game.

àfáríkɔ̀ŋ Troublesome (of

person or action). (Efik borrowing).

áfà-úkú See: **ɔ́kɔ́chị̀-úkú**

àfɔ̀ Third day of the four-day week preceding Ŋkwɔ́. **Òk'áfɔ̀**: Male child born on an àfɔ̀. **Mgb'áfɔ̀**: Female child born on an àfɔ̀.

àfɔ̀-ŋ̀sɔ̀ Third day of the four day week set aside that no one goes to work in the farms.

áfị̀fị̀ Miserly. **ónyé-**: a miserly person.

Áfịríkà Name of the African continent.

áfù Half-penny.

áfúfú (1) Punishment. (2) Suffering. **tá-**: suffer. **ùwà-**: a life of suffering. (3) Selfishness.

áfyá Market. **gbàá-**: to sell quickly. **-ŋkwɔ́**: popular market on the way to Bínvòm in Ébị̀rị̀bá. **ɔ́nu-**: price. **ónyé-**: trader. **šụ̀ú-**: lose money in trading. **tú-**: send to buy. **úlwò-**: shop. **zùú-**: buy and sell.

àgàɖá A seat, usually having four legs and a back. for one person.

àgàgḫàr̃à Big. Gigantic.

àgàjìrì A thin metal rod

with a sharp end used to hold meat, or remove items from fire.

ágálà Rabbit.

àgbà Jaw.

ágbá̱ A congenital skin disease resulting in partial or total absence of pigment.

ágbá̱ (Of disease) chronic.

ágbá̱ (Used to describe a person's attitude) that has become chronic.

àgbàlà Village square or meeting place.

ágbàlàjí A kind of Òkù yam which had been left unharvested for more than a year.

àgbà mkpɔ́kpyá Pointed Jaw

ágbáǹchị̀ Side of the face extending from the temple to the jaw.

àgbàǹkpú (1) Mumps - swelling of the salivary glands. (2) A red, wild fruit the size of a lawn tennis ball.

àgbà̱ŋgbà̱ Wash hand bowl: **-úkú**: Big enamel bowl.

ágbàríntèntè Piece of a broken earthen-ware pot. Children use smaller pieces the size of a penny to play money.

ágbáwéré Another name for **ɔ̀kpʊ̀rʊ̀kpʊ̀**

Ágbàyì Male name: Short for ágbàyị̀ghị̀ nwá ɔ́g̃u *(you do not count children).*

ágbàyị̀ghị̀ Inspite of.

àgb̯éŋ Derogatory name for a person who is hard of hearing.

Ágb̯ézè Male name.

Ágb̯ézi Short for Ágbɔ́-ezi: Name for Ńdé Òkó-ògó compound - seat of government and customary court of the Ènàchíókèn of Ébị̀rị̀bá.

ágbɔ́ Down the bottom: Towards the end.

àgbɔ̀ Gourd, Calabash: **ìkó-:** cup made from cut gourd: **ékú-:** spoon from cut gourd.

àgbɔ́ghɔ̀ Maiden: Nubile girl. **nwá-:** girl.

Ágbɔ́ña One of the communities of Ámẽ́k̃e in Ébị̀rị̀bá comprising of only Ágbɔ́ña.

Àgbɔ́ĩi See **Ègbɔ́ji**

àgbɔ̀n Native mango with a hard seed. The seed is ground to make soup slimy.

Ágbɔ́ndé Short for Ágbɔ́ ndé Òkáfɔ̀, name of a hamlet in Ámṍgùdù.

ágbɔ́-ókókó Gorge, or valley.

ágbɔ́-ókw̃ù Yam mounds usually made very high in land constantly under flood.

ágbú (1) Ulcerating sore. (2) **-nkwú:** Climbing rope.

ágbúgbá Funnel.

ághá War: **írí-:** War dance: **ŋgwá-:** Weapons of war: **ɔ́sɔ́-:** Flight from war.

ághàghị̀ Will not fail to.

ághá-Jámàn German war (Second World War).

ághàm Wolfing down. *Used in* ị̀tu -ághàm : To eat very fast.

àghàrághà Restless, troublesome (person).

àghárághara Scattered all over.

àghí Manner; condition; How? As in: *ife d' àghí* (How are things?).

ághü Monitor lizard: Iguana said to be deaf to loud sound.

ághùghɔ̀ Trickerev, as in : Ónyé ághùghɔ̀ *(a cheat: a trickster).*

àgìdì Pellets, usually from a gun cartridge.

àgìgá Needle. Pin.

ág̃u Leopard.

ág̃u-íyi Crocodile.

ág̃u-oke House rat noted

for gnawing at sleeping
people's feet while
blowing air at the site
so as not to wake its
victim.

águbá Razor.

àgwà Beans.

ágwɔ́ Snake.

ágwɔ́-mang Whitlow: An
inflammatory tumor,
especially on the
terminal phalanx of a
finger, seated between
the epidermis and true
skin.

ágwụ-ágwụ Never ending:
Cannot be depleted.

áñà That will be: as in
Áñà àkpɔ́ ya ɔ́Ḱú (*It
will be burnt*).

áñàñáŕa Edible vegetable
leaves with high
viscous properties that
sometimes do the work
of the okra in a soup. It
is slimy to the touch
when squeezed.

áñányí Extraordinarily
wonderful; Without
comparison; Never
before seen.

àñíi Rallving call (*used in:*
Àñíi Ébịŕịbá , àñíii
Ókèzyé, *to greet, hail,
or draw the attention of
a crowd or group of
people*).

áñù Discriminatory refusal
(usually of children) to
eat certain kinds of
food.

áñùmá Marks, or patterns
cut on cheeks, or
forehead as a lineage
identification.

áñútú Roasted piece of
goat underbelly usually
eaten by those who
slaughtered it.

áñw̃àá This year.

àñwékéŕé Groundnuts:
Peanuts.

àñwú Melon seed used
both to thicken food
and lend a nutty flavor
to them.

àñwú-àkpừ-àkpứ Cake
made from cooked
ground melon.

àñwùràñwù A kind of
cocoyam which must
be cooked overnight
otherwise it will itch
the throat and palate.

ájà Wooden cymbals
about a foot long and
three inches deep with
a hollow.

ájàmgbo (Said of) a girl
who takes part in
activities and games
that are more
appropriate for boys.

ájì (1) Fibre produced by
beating the back of a
certain tree and used as

loin cloth.

ájì Belt.

àjíjà Naive.

ájú-àkw̃à A traditional family shrine in the form of a pot of water out of which family members are given to drink once a year to ward off evil and ensure progress etc. Others are in the form of food cooked and every member of the family or compound eats out of it. Sometimes a small physical shrine is erected and food morsels given to it as family members eat.

ájùjú Question.

ájú-óyi Rheumatism.

àK̃á (1) Next year. (2) History.

ákáchì Completely dried corn.

ákaghaka Not ripe or strong (especially fruits - not ready for harvesting).

ákà-ghí (Expression, meaning) You don't say!

ákàghílé Derogatory name for one (usually a child) who would not follow instructions or advice.

Ákáñàbá One of the thirteen age-grades in Ɛ́bírìbá.

àK̃áñì Last year.

ákánchu Whip: Cane for whipping.

Àkàñdèm Traditional dance of the Ámõgùdù community in Ɛ́bírìbá.

ákánkpɔ Ring worm. Lichen.

Àkánu One of the thirteen age-grades in Ɛ́bírìbá.

àkàrà Ground-beans fritters.

àkàràchúchú See **ákánchu.**

ákàrà-ɛ́kà Fate; destiny.

àkàràsì Liquor glass

ákárilù A crunchy, bitter, fruit seed eaten raw and used with kola nuts to present to visitors.

àkáwá Potash - used to curdle oil for eating or to tenderize tough, cooked animal skin.

áK̃ì Nut: Palm kernel nut.

áK̃ì-áñàñáṝa Painful lymph node usually in the groin and armpit following a wound.

áK̃ì-àkwárì Nut produced by a wild climbing plant which tastes like the palm kernel nut

áK̃ì-bèkeé Coconut.

áK̃ì-ḿkpúŋkpú Kidney.

ákị̀rị̀ Side of the body:
Ribs.

ákị̀rị̀-éhwɔ Intestines:
Innards.

ákị̀rị̀-ényi Another name
for the wooden
clappers used by
traditional war dancers.
Originally the clappers
were fashioned out of
the ribs of an elephant.
It also has the
onomatopoeic name:
kwàá-kwàá-chị̌

ákị̀rị̀syà Clams. Oysters.

ákị̀sị̀ Scarf.

àkɔ́ Smart: Cunning:
Common Sense: Clever.

ákpá-àlị̀ (Of language)
indigenous; existing in
a place from the
earliest known times.

àkpàghàrà Beetle with a
hard proboscis found
mostly on cut palm
trees: -íshí nkɔm: A
variant of the beetle
with its proboscis
curved back and shaped
like a spoon;
Rhinoceros beetle.

ákpàghárá Side of the
body from the shoulder
to the waist.

ákpá-ị̀fè Off color

ákpájímá One of the
figures (usually a man
dressed as a woman)

during the Úgú
Ɔkàgwó festivals of the
Ègbɔ́ji community.
The figure is usually
beautiful and the name
is sometimes used to
describe a beautiful
woman.

àkpàK̃àr̃à Bench made by
strapping several
bamboo sticks in a row.

àkpàkóró Mollusk - a
kind of snail with white
shell found mostly in
fresh waters.

ákpárá Palm tree fronds
with the leaves
removed.

àkpàràjà Any large
matchet.

àkpàráwà Young man:
Stalwart boy. (Efik
borrowing).

ákpárí-ékèghì-érírí
Vcgetable leaves which
stick to each other
when squeezed so that
no strings are needed to
tie them.

ákpị̀ Members of the
genus arachnid
including spiders,
scorpion and mites.

ákpị̀kpá Much talk, as in:
ónyé-: talkative person.

ákpị̀kpị̀ Scorpion.

ákpị̀kpị̀ (Of a person with
a habit of) miserliness.

30

ákpúghúrí Grub, or the larva of the àkpàghàrà beetle found in decaying palm trees. -:òtùlà-ágbá A long darker variant of grub.

ákpúkpɔ́ Hide, Skin, Leather.

ákpúkpɔ́-ɔ́kpà Shoes.

ákpúkpɔ́-áʈu Hide from a buffalo.

àkpùlù Edible fig-like fruit the side of a ping-pong ball. -íyí máng: Derogatory description for unusually large eyeballs.

àkpùràkpú A poor imitation.

àkpùrákpù Ankle.

ákpúru Seed. Nut.

ákpúru-ʈkpákpà Corn kernel; grain.

ákpúru-úkà The main points.

ákú Arrow.

àkù Flying termites, usually edible that appear at the onset of the rainy season and are attracted to bright lights at night at which they lose their wings in the morning.

áƘúmáƘú Plants.

àkùmákù Guess work.

àkùpé Hand held fan usually made of woven raffia.

àkùrù A kind of yam.

ákwà Outside, Aside, Apart.

ákw̃ákw̃á A kind of tree with soft wood used mostly in making cheap coffins.

ákw̃árà (1) Root, as in ákw̃árà ósísí. (2) Tendon, as in ákw̃árà ánù ..

àkwári A kind of climbing plant used as rope.

àkwàtánkwà Sticks for playing instruments: Drumsticks.

ákw̃ú Cotton wood tree that grows to a great height.

àkw̃ùkw̃à (1) Foot bridge. (2) (Of persons) prone to accidents.

àlàwàrà A kind of dwarf palm tree that can be harvested standing on the ground.

àlɪ Land. -èzí: land belonging to everybody in the compound. -íkwú: land belonging to members of an extended family. -ɔ́ñà: land belong to everybody.

àlɪ-ádì-ápá (Literally) It is difficult to lift the land. Nickname given to a difficult person.

Àl̩í-ézé-Chíneké
Kingdom of God.
Heaven.

ál̩ìká Name, as in (ál̩ìká èchàrà) used to describe èchàrà which is no longer soft for cooking soup.

ál̩ìlà Centipede.

ál̩ìm From íta al̩ìm - kind of punishment meted out to someone defeated in a game of àsà involving the punching of the open hand of the loser placed on a bed of sand.

ál̩ì-ńgbahi Farm land left fallow which has become ready for cultivation again.

áñá Path. Road leading into a compound. Open space. A kind of arena. A gathering point. **-έ mang:** (Meeting place of the spirits) used to indicate an unusually far distance.

àma Know-it-all.

àmà Revelation, as in ígba àmà (*to reveal*).

àmádi Wealthy person. Contented person. Noble.

Àmá-ebya One of the subdivisions in Egboji

comprising Ezi Elu, Ńdé Okorye. Ezi Iyieru, Ŋ́dé Okefi, Ŋ́dé Okerezi, and Nde Icho.

Àmá-elu One of the subdivisions in Egbojĩ comprising Ńdé Dikẽ, Ńdé Uko, Ŋ́dé Mbị̀la, Ńdé Agwu, Ŋ́dé Obya, Ŋ́dé Ekpu, and Ezi Agbɔ́.

ámàghị̀ Ignorance. No knowledge. Unknown.

ámaghì-èyè A very long time; Unknown, or uncountable number of time period.

Áñájа One of the eleven subdivisions of Áñék̃e in Ɛ́bíríbá comprising Ńdé Ị̃si, Ŋ́dé Oléɔ̀gū, Ŋ́dé Mgbíkere, Ŋ́dé Okéῆé, Ŋ́dé Egbe, and Ŋ́dé Ù̩wànu.

ámàmá Well known.

Áñámbà One of the subdivisions of Áñógùdù in Ɛ́bíríbá comprising of Ńdé Ezérà. Ŋ́dé Niɔ̀kū, Ŋ́dé Udéɔ̀gù, Ŋ́dé Uchenta, Ŋ́dé Enwãrã. Ńdé Irukwu. Agbɔ̀-ŋ́dé-Okafɔ̀, and Ɔ̀zwã divided into Ŋ́dé Okóró, and Ŋ́dé Ngèlé.

Áñántà One of the eleven subdivisions of

Áméǩe in Ébíríbá comprising Ńdé Uchè, Ńdé Olòló. Ńdé Ɔ́lùghù, Ńdé Ɔ́tìsì. Ŋ́dé Ichɔ. Ńdé Agbàyì, Ŋ́dé Obu, Ŋ́dé Okórìgwò, Ŋ́dé Okor'emang. Agb'ezi Okpocha. Ńdé Ɔ́kuwa. Ńdé Okewu, and Ŋ́dé Ɛ́nya-égwu.

ámámfyã Gingivitis. Toothache.

àmàmí̃fé Wisdom. Smart. The knowledge of something.

ámàr̃ì Known.

Áméǩbelù One of the eleven subdivisions of Áméǩe in Ébíríbá comprising Ńdé Odìm, Ńdé Okpo. Agbɔ́ Ivieru, Ŋ́dé Ugbɔ́eia. Ńdé Oti, Agbo Ɔ́ii. Ŋ́dé Ɛ́bam, Ńdé Okpóròkpóta, and Ŋ́dé Otẽ.

Áméǩe One of the three main divisions of the Ébíríbá community which include Áméǩe-Echichi, Ihũngwù, Úmúesõ, Ihébu, Áméãja, Áméǩbelu, Áméántà, Ukpo, Binyòm, Agbɔ́hà, and Áméúbá.

Áméǩe-echíchì One of the subdivisions of Áméǩe in Ébíríbá comprising Ŋ́dé Erim (divided

into Ŋ́dé Ebèdé and Ńdé Irúkè). Ńdé Ɔ́nùma, Ŋ́dé Áméã-Ńta. Ńdé Áméã-úkú. Ńdé Okó Ɔ́nwu, Ŋ́dé Chiɔkpɔ. Ńdé Okogo. and Ŋ́dé Ɔ́núkpu-Ŋ́ta.

àmị̀ Female.

ámì Straw.

ámímvã Rafters.

ámi-nkɔ́lɔ̀ Windpipe.

Áméògùdù One of the three main divisions of the Ébíríbá community comprising, Úmúechukwu, Údantà, Amámbà, and Ogbu.

ámù Scrotum.

Áméúbá One of the eleven subdivisions of Áméǩe in Ébíríbá comprising Ŋ́dé Okórónkwo, Ńdé Emèwu, Ezi-elu, Ŋ́dé Ebẽ, Nde Iròùwà, Nde Ali-Ukwú, Ŋ́dé Okpukpu, and Ŋ́dé Okwo.

Áméúkú Central arena in Áméǩe where the Ébíríbá annual wrestling match is held and where the ruling Ènàchíòkèn stands to pass the enacted laws of the land to the age grade in charge of its implementation.

ámúméã Thunder.

ámúmá Prophecy, as in: íbu ámúmá *(to prophesy).*

àmùmà Shine. Reflect, as in a lightning.

àmúmù Cowardice. Weakness.

ámúžù Place of sojourn. **nwá-:** sojourner.

Ámúžù-Béndĕ Abiriba sojourners who lived around the old Bende division of Eastern Nigeria stretching to Port Harcourt.

áŋa Cane.

ánàghúkwà Bicycle. (Efik borrowing).

áŋàřà A kind of egg-plant that can be eaten raw, usually presented with kola nuts to visitors.

ani Alone. Only. As in: *ónyé-ani* (person alone)

áníní Quarter of a penny.

ánòghù Absent.

ánú Meat. Animal. Beast.

ánú-byáǹkó Meat of unknown origin.

ánú-érírí See òlógbù-óko.

ánú-éžì Pork.

ánú-ħwú Flesh.

ánù-námà Beef.

ánù-mànù animal; beast; stupid person

ánù-mgbóko *(Bush animal)* Derogatory name for a stupid person

ánú-ófya Bush meat. Also a derogatory name for a stupid person.

ánú-ókwùrù Uncut okra dropped in a vegetable soup and used as meat.

ánw̃u Sun.

ánw̃u-ánw̃u Never dying; immortal.

ánw̃untà A small, greyish antelope-like animal.

Ányám Stream in Ámĕřke.

ányí We. Us.

ányì Large quantity.

àpàpá (Used to describe) a child carried in the hands; as in *M' àpàpá, m'èsèsè* (including children carried, and those held at hand, but walking alongside.

àpàtà Thigh, Lap.

àpàtàngbùghúdú A species of water leaf with tiny leaves.

àpàtúkú A kind of large banana or plantain.

àpìrì-àpì Castrated he-goat.

ápìrìpá-òkpù Buttocks.

áráħá-agakwa A kind of mushroom said to be so good you want to go for seconds.

árámárá The act of eating sweets, fruits, food, etc.

àrí Parasitic worm that

lives in and attacks eyes.

àrírá Catfish

árírí-éƙá Intestinal worm.

árìryɔ́ Begging; request, prayer; plea.

áru (1) Abomination. (2) Aberration, Wound, Dent, Bruise.

árúrú-àlì Act of mischief; wickedness; meanness.

árwà (1) Spear. (2) The two pieces of cut bamboo sticks that form the skeleton to thatch mats.

áryá Personal or household belongings.

ásá A kind of flat fish of the Tilapia species usually smoke-dried.

àsà A kind of game.

ás̃á Cheek.

ás̃á-ŋ́di Cut yam pieces used as seedling.

ás̃á-ŋ́púnpú Round, big cheeks

àsábɔ̀ A traditional dance of the Úmùés̃ò community in which a small, square heavily decorated cloth hut with a stuffed python on the top is carried around.

àsí A kind of multi-colored stringed ornamental beads

usually worn by women around the waist or neck; sometimes strung together and laced in rows to form a skirt worn by maidens.

àsị Strong dislike, or hatred.

àsíkɔ̀ŋ Tobacco. (Efik borrowing).

àsímewɔ̀ Spawn (eggs of toads).

àsịntà-ńdé-óru Plant producing bead-like seeds found mostly in river banks.

ásùsú Language.

átá A black, foul-smelling ant.

átághílé A kind of mushroom that is sometimes difficult to chew.

átáŋ Clock, bell.

átáŋ-ɛ́kà Wrist-watch.

àtànkàrà Traditional dance in a long flowing robe topped with an animal skull or the like and known to chase women and children.

átú Chisel used mostly by palm wine tapsters.

át̃ú Buffalo.

át̃ú Traditional dance with égwɔ̀ skirt and an animal skull on the head.

átù Small projection at the top of the rump of a hen usually cut off when the hen becomes sick.

átụ-égw̃ù Fearless. Intrepid.

àtùkpú Unpleasant after effects of excessive eating; indigestion.

àtùmà Giant catfish (Shark).

átù-ɔ́kpà Heel; Achilles tendon.

átúřu Lamb.

átùtù Clitoris.

áwáɗà A kind of yam.

àwàkísɔ̀ng Giant umbrella. (Efik borrowing).

àwálowò A species of flowering shrub (*Eupatorium Odorata*). It is an aromatic shrub, covered in fine grey hairs. The shrub is named after Chief Obafemi Awolowo whose helicopter spread campaign flyers in the area in the 1960s and the plant appeared for the first time.

Á.W.C.O Abiriba Women Cultural Organization with the aim to uplift women.

Áwúsá Hausa: Name given to all the northern people of Nigeria.

àyàwùrù Large; Big.

áyíghá Dysentery.

àyúm Onions.

ázà (1) Stunted, Short. (2) Tribal marks.

àzígo A kind of board game with twelve holes or grooves sometimes dug on the earth played by two persons with palm kernel nuts, seeds or small stones.

áz̃ù Fish.

àz̃ú Back. Rear.

áz̃ù-cháŋ Canned-fish.

àz̃úmà A kind of local brown and black coloured beans in a long pod.

àzw̃à Cut tree stems used for building mud-walled houses.

b

B Second letter of the alphabet.

Ɓá (1) Boast, as in: Íɓa mɓa *(to boast)*. (2) Peel, as in: Íɓa ńdí *(to peel yam)*. (3) Be initiated (into a cult or secret society). (4) Grab.

bá Be rich and wealthy, as in Íba úbá *(to be rich and wealthy)*.

bághá-bàghà-bághà Spread flat.

Ɓàndé Catch; Grab; hold down.

Ɓányí Make a bold a statement or threaten.

Ɓànyí Enter.

Ɓànyísa Come inside.

bàrà-bàrà *Used to describe Urine, rain or water* spewing like a jet.

Ɓàr̃ị Get into trouble because of.

Ɓà-úrù Important.

Ɓé Yell, as in: Yá ɓe *(he yelled)*.

bèbé To lean something on.

bèchwó Make worthless by touching or perching on.

bédébèdè Aimless sauntering

bèé-ịnyàŋ (Of fish) in the early process of decay, or affected by rot. (Efik borrowing).

Ɓèé Peel (orange).

bèghè-bèghè Lax (grip). Loose (knot).

bèkéè White man; English man; English language.

bèkéè -hwú úzɔ̀ lwá ìgbò: Albino.

bèjwó (Of birds, insects etc.,) flocking together.

Ɓé'nyá "Go into the eyes" as in, intoxicate.

bèríbe Brightly multicoloured beetle also called June beetle.

bèyí Perch.

bí Cut, as in: Bìyím ánú *(cut me a piece of meat)*.

bịbịr̃ịr̃ị Thickly greasy (to the touch).

bíbyèé Ruin. Destroy.

bíƙo Please.

Bínyòm One of the subdivisions of Ámᷠéƙe in Ɛ́bíríbá comprising of Íŋdé Aghàm, Íŋdé Udẽ. Íŋdé Ekom, and Íŋdé Oryentàwhich is also known as Eziúkwú.

bìtú Touch, mostly with the hands and fingers.

bú *(Suffix)* break off, as in: Gbú bùú *(cut off)*.

bù Be, Is, as in: Bù máɗù *(is somebody)*.

bù Reside.

bùrú Carry.

bùrú Uproot.

búpù Carry off.

bùsíbé Go down (on one's knees).

bùsíñá Bear the brunt of (usually a wrong).

bùtɔ́ Fell (a tree) by uprooting.

bùú Carry (bear). **-éhwɔ́ íme:** be pregnant. **-ághá:** wage war. **-ámúmá:** prophesy. **-ɗàá:** put own. **-ghá:** lift past. **-lyé:** lift up. **-kwàsì:** lift to. **-óbù:** bear in mind. **-pù:** lift off.

formal consent is given for the marriage.

bwɔ́ To appear or become visible.

bwɔ́-enya Pull open the eyelid as a form of disparagement.

bwɔ́ɔ́ (1) To gut - remove the intestines. as in: Bwɔ́ɔ́ ánù *(gut an animal)*. (2) The process of weeding with a how, as in: Ìbwɔ ɛfífyá *(weeding)*. (3) Break (of day), as in:

bùú Uproot, as in: Ìbù íwá *(to harvest cassava by uprooting)*.

bùú Be fat, as in: Bùú íbù *(be fat)*.

bwá Spit in spray.

bwã Find (lost item). Discover.

bwà-bwà *Used to describe*: any liquid uncontrollably spilling from its container.

bwághá-bwághá Gregarious; Lively, amicable, and boisterous (of person).

bwó (1) Put a load (on somebody). (2) Accuse falsely. (3) Come to an end; terminate.

bwó-mànyì Presentation of drinks to a bride's family at which time Chí bwɔ́ɔ́ *(when the day breaks)*. (4) Open (by pulling apart), as in: Bwɔ́ɔ́ ɛ̀kpà *(open a bag)*.

bwɔ́ɔ́ chí Day breaks.

bwɔ́-ɔ̀kpù To moon, or bare the buttocks as an act of insult.

bwɔ́pù (1) Pay court costs. (2) Take off with speed (as in a race).

bwɔ̀wá Pull apart by hand.

byá Come, as in: Byá ɛ́báà *(come here)*.

bỹá (1) Press down. (2) Print.

byàkwá Ensure that you come; be sure to come.

byé Slice; Cut to pieces, as in: Byé ɔ́kwừrừ *(cut up the okra).*

bỹe-ɔ́mà Hug.

byépàrí To step on, as in: Byépàrí nsḧi *(to step in faeces).*

ch

ch Diagraph pronounced at the first syllable of "church".

chá No (emphatic).

chñá Ripen.

chñà Of a particular color; have the color of.

chàá (1) Dredge; (2) cut (a length of cloth).

chàbwɔ́ Of cloth (lose color); fade.

chàgháryá Change color; lose original color.

chàyì Exclamation equivalent to "my goodness" used mostly to express surprise or consternation.

chánìyà Canned fish. (Efik borrowing).

cháŋ Iron sheet; tin, zinc.

ché Guard.

chèbé Protect; keep guard over.

chèchñínyé Wait in ambush.

chèé Think.

chèé-échìchè Give a serious thought; contemplate.

chèéri Think for

chèèri Make (a baby) drink.

chègháryá Think differently. Change one's mind.

chèrí (1) Support, as in: Chèrí ísì *(support the head)* as with a pillow. (2) Collect (water) from a tap etc.

chèmbé Depend upon. Hope on.

chèsá Remember.

chètú Wait.

chètúrú Give (a baby or child) water to drink.

chí A god

chí Day, as in: Chí bwɔ̀ *(day break),* and: Chí jyé *(night fall).*

chñí (1) Block, as in: Úzɔ̀ chñí *(the road is blocked).* (2) To rub off.

chñị Become dull (of sharp object).

chị Rule. Lead, as in: ɔ̀chíchí *(rulership, leadership).*

chị To be slippery.

chìí Crack (palm kernet nuts)

chñì Laugh.

chịpú Haul away

chịpụ́ụ́ (Of clothing or other items) no longer in vogue.

chíchíchí Grasshoper.

chícħìr̃ì (In dipping a soup, or sauce), the act of scraping the bottom of the plate or pot, (especially when there is not enough soup. or sauce.)

chícħir̃ír̃í (Of woven items) tight and close together.

chìkátá Gather; bring together; pack together; (of speech) summarize.

chìm To be straight and perfect.

Chíneke̖ God the creator (Almighty).

chí-ɔjɔ́ɔ: Hard luck *(bad god)*.

chìrí Collect and take.

chíríbwɔ́m A form of sexually transmitted disease characterized by the formation of a painful, purulent cyst on the groin area. Bubo in the groin.

chìtá Crack and eat (palm kernel nuts).

cħìtụ́ Touch mostly with body.

chí–uku: *(See* **Chúkú***)*.

cħòbé Arrange.

cħòó Levv. as in: Cħòó wá pɔ́n ábwɔ̀ *(levy them two Pounds)*.

chɔ́ Want. Desire. Seek, as in:

chɔ́chɔ́chɔ́ A kind of insect

chɔ́ghá To go looking for something, or someone.

chɔ́-ńma: beautify.

chɔ́-ùɗó: seek for peace.

chɔ́-ụ́kà: look for trouble; start a fight.

chɔ́pụsá Discover; Find out.

chɔ́sá Find; search for.

chụ Pursue. **-ɔ́sɔ́:** chase. **-pụ:** chase off. **-ńtá:** hunt.

chú (1) Fetch (water). (2) Be tarnished, or faded. (3) Something expected to happen but did not happen, as in: **-ụ́r̃á:** Be sleepless.

cħú Offer, as in : Cħú èjà *(offer in sacrifice)*.

Chúkú: big god *(God almighty)*.

chụ́sàá chase off (people, or animals) in various directions.

chụ́cħw̃àá Brush back and forth, as in: Chụ́cħw̃àa ɔ́nu àlì *(to*

41

have one's mouth brushed on the ground) as a form of punishment.

chwàá Chase; drive out or away; dismiss.

chyé (1) Shout. (2) Crack, as in: Chyé áⱩí *(crack a kernel).*

chỹé Become blocked, impassable.

chyé Scream, or raise an alarm.

chyé-ḿkpú Shout, or raise alarm.

d

dá Warm. Make hot. Scald.

ɗàá (1) Land, or Fall (to the ground. (2) Be afflicted with (an ailment). (3) Sound, as in: Dàá ụ́ɗà *(make a sound)*.

ɗàá-ɛ́ɗà: To fall

ɗàá-íbì: Be afflicted with hydrocele.

ɗàá-iwu: break the law.

ɗàá-m̀bà: Faint. Feel faint because of hunger.

ɗàá-ŋgwúru: Be lame.

ɗàá-òbóm: Become subserviently greedy.

ɗàá-ógbèvì: Be poor.

ɗàá-ùkɔ̀rɔ̀: Become indigent.

ɗáɓà Fall into.

dàch̃ýé Block planned event; intervene; obstruct.

ɗàgbúh̃ú Fall to the ground.

ɗàgbwó Fall on (and crush to death).

ɗàj̃úh̃ú Be calm. Be cool.

ɗànɗé Fall against.

dám-dám Sparkling, giving off light, as in: Ìke dám-dám *(to be sparkling)*.

dàrị̀ Formerly.

Previously.

dé Lay in a row (as of cement block).

dèbé Put. Keep.

dèch̃ýé Replace. Apply (dressing).

dédém A light, almost imperceptible (touch).

dédùú (Washed items) not done right.

dèghèdèghè Soft.

dènɗé Put against.

dètụ́ Touch with a dab (of medical ointment).

dèyì Cold.

dèyí Soak. Prepare by adding hot water, as in: Dèyí gàrí *(prepare garri)*.

dèyì-dèyì Damp.

dì Be. Ìs. (In a state of).

díbyà Doctor. Physician. Medicine man. Also, native doctor.

dì-égw̃ù Be frightening.

dì-ɛ́nyà Be distant, or far off.

dj̃h̃í Get well (from illness or poverty).

dì-ích̃ò Be different.

dì-íme Be pregnant.

dìkàtà Similar. Alike.

dík̃e Be powerful, as in Nwók̃e dík̃e *(strong*

or powerful man). Male name.

dímgba Champion wrestler. Male name.

dímkpà Adult male.

dì-m̀kpà Is important.

dì-ńdù Be alive.

dì-ńkɔ́ Be sharp.

dì-ńma Is beautiful.

dì-ǹswó Be near.

dínta Master hunter.

di-ɔ́k̃é-ɔ́nu Be very expensive.

dìrị̀ Be with.

ɖó Talk heatedly (especially when upset).

ɖó-ŋ̀tó Betray by telling, or ratting on.

ɖònyí Rat on. Betray.

ɖòó-ɛ́nyà Make clear. Clarify. Understand.

ɖòsí Scold.

ɖòr̃ú See **ɖòtú.**

ɖòtú Dip (especially morsel of food) in soup or stew.

dɔ́ Pull.

dɔ́-bùrú cut a piece.

dɔ́-gbwó Pull to kill.

dɔ́-kàá Tear.

dɔ́-kásyá tear into pieces.

dɔ́-wáá tear apart.

dɔ̀ɔ́ Draw. Pull.

dɔ̀ɔ́-ɛká-ńcħì: Warn. Advice (by pulling the ear).

dɔ̀kásyá Tear into pieces.

dɔ̀lη̃ A kind of ointment

for massaging painful swellings.

dɔ̀rụ́ (of water, or wine in a large pot) sitting motionless.

dụ́ Jam. Bump.

dùbá Dress (someone).

dúɓàá Lead (someone) into.

dùgbwó Kill by hanging.

dùghá Sit

dùghá-ɔ́dì Sit down.

dúħwùú Mislead.

dúkw̃àá See (a visitor) off.

dùlàá (1) (Of girls) give out in marriage. (2) Send home.

dụ́pụ̀ Undress; remove (clothing item)

dùrú Sit.

dụ́rụ̀ Dress up

dùú Escort. Accompany. - pùú: see off. -lá: accompany home.

ɖùú Prick. Probe. Jab.

dụ̀ụ́-ɔ́nú-ɛ́gbɔ Provoke vomit

dụ̀yí Come to a stop (of vehicles). Berth (of boats).

dùyí (1) Send. (2) Pass a rope around (to tie).

dw̃àá (1) Sew; (2) counsel, as in: dw̃àá ɔ̀dɔ́ *(give advice).*

dwòó (Of rain) fall

dwɔ̀ɔ́ Scramble, or struggle for;

dwɔ̀rṹ To take, or get
something for self,
usually when fair
sharing is not possible.
dwɔ̀rṹ-ṳ̀wà (*Tighten a
loin wrap*). Used to
describe a preparedness
for something that is
going to happen.
dwɔ̀yị̂ Transplant
(especially seedling).

e

é In, At, as in: É'lu (*at the top*).

ébe See ébe-ntà-òrindi.

ébé About.

ébébé (Of a person) acting or behaving in a cantankerous manner.

èbérè Forgiveness.

ébélébé Full of shock, wonder and surprises; Marvelous.

ébèm A kind of raffia palm - the fronds and stalk of which tend to be unusually sharp and containing thorns.

èbèŋgó The most colorful of the two ɔ́kɔ́ŋkɔ̀-átáng masquerades of the Ébịrịbá -ùmɔ́n.

ébe-ńtà-òríndi Yam beetle.

ébì Porcupine.

Ébìrì Another name for Ègbɔ́ji.

ébítàlì Giant bush rat.

èbù (1) Mold. (2) Wasp. Hornet.

èbù-ị̃ji A kind of yellow insect the size of a house-fly but with the sting of a bee.

èbùbè Wonder.

èbùlù Ram.

ébúrú Age mates.

échí Tomorrow.

échìchè Thought.

èchìchì Middle. Centre.

èchíchì-àbàlị Midnight.

édú (1) Small animal of the rodent family known for its constant sleeping. (2) Derogatory name for a sleepy head.

èé-èghé Public outcry and protest usually by women against abominable acts. The name taken from the cry of the women protesters: èé-èghéè! èé-èghé!

èfè Hang without touching the ground.

éfè Chance.

èfètéfè (Hanging) mid-air

éfï Cow; bull.

égbé Hawk. Kite.

égbè Gun. Rifle.

égbè-élígwó Mildew.

égbélé-ńkwà A small, hand-held animal skin drum used mostly to announce the death of a titled man.

égbé-ògùgù Elephant grass.

égbè-ɔ́kwa Home made shot gun.

égbérè Wooden hoe handle.

égbérégbé Board used for cutting up meat.

égbérùg̃ò (Of a person carried) shoulder high.

égbùrègbú Vegetable for eating yam, prepared by cutting up boiled leaves on a wooden board.

ègègé Swing, as in: Ịtu ègègé (*to swing back and forth*).

ég̃è A kind of broad leaves used specially for wrapping èsụ̀sụ́.

èghèrèghé Fried (food item).

èghórò Appeal. Begging. Apology.

èghórò-ónyé íƘe: The apology of an unrepentant person.

ègú Caterpiller with black hairy covering that feeds on vegetation

ègwéyí Fishing hook.

égw̃ù Fear.

égw̃ù-átu Intrepid; Fearless.

égwùgwù Rainbow.

éh̃é Pubic area.

éh̃wùré African nutmeg.

èh̃wùrù High,

èjìmá Twins.

éjù See **éjùjù**

éjùjù Broken earthen ware used mostly for roasting groundnuts and *àz̃úmà*.

éƘé Python.

èƘé One of the four Igbo market days following ŋkwó.

ékè Any personal peculiarity, mannerism, etc. Idiosyncrasy.

èƘélè Greetings.

èƘémbu Ɛ́bị́rị́bá traditional New Yam's Day. The first èƘé which marks the beginning of the new yam day celebration. Usually a day of merriment involving the cooking and eating of new yam for the first time in the year.

éƘéřè A kind of string from fibre strands taken from palm fronds used mostly for tending yam.

ékésù Top.

èkèténshi Literally "Basket of poison;" Name for a group of traditional medicine practitioners.

éƘíƘé Amulet; talisman.

ékìké Creation.

éƘò (1) Blacksmith's bellows. (2) Gizzard.

ékpe Death-bed wish; last words of a dying person.

ékpè All-male traditional dance characterized by the *ékpè* making a mooing sound.

èkpè-Béndẽ Traditional *ékpè* society associated with the ama-uzu Bende.

èkpè-éK̃a "Tall masquerage" is traditional dance of the Áñúbá community of Ébịrịbá characterized by a baby-looking being in a tall crown hat raised on a very long pole.

èkpè-ékɔrɔ Traditional dance of the Ùkᴅó community of Ébịrịbá characterized by a masquerade in èkɔ́rɔ climbing plant costume chase people about and try to scratch their bodies with razor-sharp wɔ́ɔ̀wɔ́ɔ̀ and ékpètére stems.

ékpékansi Of a woman usually in a hurry in speech, acts, and demeanor.

ékpém Bottle. (Efik borrowing).

èkpèntá Leprosy.

èkpérè Prayers.

ékpètére A thorny climbing plant in the bush.

ékpè- úmúr̃ìmá Ékpè play exclusively for children. The children build a palm frond ékpè hut and make ékpè sounds in the hut, and finally go into a plantain cluster to harvest some which they cook around the hut to eat.

ékpiri Dancing costume piece made by stringing cut pieces of shells of a large dried nut and usually tied around the ankle or held in hand to sound in time with the dancers' moves.

ékpó Masquerade. Mask (Efik borrowing).

ékú Large spoon. Ladle.

éK̃ùK̃ófo First faeces of a new born baby.

ékwénsu Satan; Devil - god of mischief.

ékwó A hand-held, hollowed-out wooden instrument; slit wooden gong.

ékwó-ŋgba Traditional wrestling music.

ékw̃ú Hearth. Stove.

ékw̃ù The neck back of

the head.

Èkwùu Traditional secret society in Ébịríbá.

élé Antelope.

élée If we look.

éleghiji A strong smelling dried fish used as seasoning.

èléyi Where?

élìlì Melons.

élɔ́ Discharged placenta after birth.

élu Up; top; surface

élu-y'àlì: Heaven and earth.

élu-ụ̀wà: On earth.

élu-ígwo: Sky. Heaven.

èlù Oil produced by frying palm kernel nuts.

èlù-áƘí: palm nut oil.

èlù-éƘé: python's fat.

émé After.

émḗñá Afterwards.

émeře Fibre from the palm tree fronds used to make rope.

émúmé Stream in Bínyòm in Ébịríbá.

émùmé Behaviour.

èním̀bwɔ́ A kind of cocoyam.

ènwò Monkey.

énwòghụ̀ Lacking

ényí Elephant.

ényì Friend.

ényí-mini Hippopotamus.

ènyò Mirror. Glass.

èpèlé Draughts (checkers).

éreghere Absolute last price

éřegheře (Defunct language of Ɔ̀gbụ̀ for) Afternoon.

èrèkèrè-m̀búba Butterfly; Moth.

érénkéŋké-èba Supine position. Lying down face up.

èrí See **érírí**

èrí-íƘe-ìsì Hair-plaiting thread.

èríkàyíkɔ́ Vegetable soup made with a mixture of pumpkin leaves and water leaves. (Efik borrowing).

érímérí Food.

érímérí-àbàlì Dinner.

Èrínma One of the age grades in Ébịríbá.

érírí Rope. String. Thread.

érírí-ŋ́kwú Palm climber's rope.

èrú A pair of traditional masquerades with beautiful face masks and skirts of folded pieces of cloth. Also a name for an unusually beautiful woman.

èrùrù Electric fish.

èrúka Pin worm - a parasitic worm found in the rectum of man, especially children causing a lot of itching

around the anal
opening.

érwó Mushroom. Fungi.

érwó-ɛ́bábì A kind of bird.

érwó-ńgbáwá A kind of
mushroom said to taste
like chicken.

érwó-ɔ̀chì A specie of
hallucinogenic
mushroom.

ésè Any of various animal
sound.

èsè Question; inquiry, as
in: *júrú èsè* (make
inquiries) usually in
connection with
diviners.

èsèsè (Used to describe) a
child held at hand, but
walking alongside.
See:**àpàpá**.

èsín An animal-skin drum
made in the shape of a
pot with three legs and
played with sticks.

ésísí Trouble that one
accidentally falls into.

ésṹ Millipede.

èté Honorific term used
alone or with a name to
call a male person older
than the call. (Efik
borrowing).

ètè-ɔ́kpà The hamstring at
the tope of a human
heel.

étére Broad leaves used in
wrapping èsùsù.

ètèrèkísɔng Urn with
three legs used for
cooking (Efik
borrowing).

étu Leech.

étùtúru Hiccups.

éwo Oh!

éwú Goat. Also used to
describe a stupid
person, as in: Ị̀bụ éwú
(you are stupid).

èyé Including. Plus.

éyè *Used in:* Ítu éyè *(to
enact and present laws).*
The act in which the
Ɛ̀nàchíòkèn of Ɛ́bíríbá
presents the yearly
mores governing the
people.

éze Tooth. Teeth.

ézè King.

ézè-ezi Traditional ruler of
the compound.

éze-ɛ̀kpí Dirty teeth.

ézè-nwami Queen.

éze-ǹpú ɛ̀bwɔ̀ Double
growing teeth.

éze-ògó Traditional ruler
of a village section.

éze-ògóm Buck-tooth.

éze-ókóghóró Missing
teeth.

éze-òmùmé Tooth-ache.

éze-órélá Rotten teeth.

éze-úzɔ̀ gap-toothed.

ézè-ɔ́kpà The big toe.

ézí Good. Quality. Real.

ézí-maɖụ Good person

éžì Pig.

èzí Outside. Compound.

ézí-ɛ́kà Right hand.

èzí-ɛ́nyásì Night vigil.

ézí-ŋ́di Yam (*Dioscorea Rotundata*).

ézí-ʊ́kà True; Truth.

ézíya Authentic. Real. In truth.

ézìzì (1) Mole. (2) **íri:-** Sensitive (to light or touch).

Ɛ

ɛ̀' To.

ɛ́ In, At, as in: Ɛ́'ħwɔ́ (*in the stomach*).

ɛ́báà Here.

Ɛ́bàm Southern neighbours of the Ɛ́bịrịbá

ɛ̀bántà-élígwo A bird family known as Swallows.

ɛ̀bïbàrà Wall.

Ɛ́bịrịbá A town in Abia State of Nigeria. The people and their language.

ɛ́ɓú́ Pus. Yellowish discharge from an infected wound.

ɛ́ɓụ̀ Armpit.

ɛ́bụ̀ Song.

ɛ́ɓú́-àlï A venomous snake ; adder; viper.

ɛ̀ɓụ̀ɓà Fat or fatty tissue.

ɛ́bú́bà Feather.

ɛ́ɓú́ɓụ̀ Pounded palm nut fibre left after the removal of the kernels.

ɛ́bú́ghú́rí-ŋkpɛ̀m̀kpɛ̀ One of a group of masquerades of the Ɛ́bịrịbá-Béndè dance with a large amount of égwɔ́ as costume making it unusually fat.

ɛ́bụ́lí Swollen. Any part of a human body swollen out of proportion.

ɛ̀bwɔ́ Formerly plantation, or wooded area of a settlement as the early developed residential parts of Ɛ́bịrịbá.

ɛ̀bwɔ́ɔ Two.

ɛ́byábu Secret society in Ɛ́bịrịbá characterized by a half-naked man holding a contraption on a long stick which he throws in the air.

ɛ̀bỹanyi Visit.

ɛ́chàghàrì Chaff.

ɛ̀chàrà The soft part of the elephant grass used for cooking soup.(*Pennistum purpucem*)

ɛ̀chịchãr̃à Biscuit. Bread. Any flour based baked item.

ɛ̀chịchị Left over burnt wood and twigs after a cut forest had been set on fire.

èdjíkj̀ (Eat food) without stew or soup.

èdà Curds thrown up by babies.

ɛ́dà Fall.

ɛ́dám Oar. Paddle.

ɛ́dʉ Species of yam plant producing yam tubers on the branches.

ɛ́dú-ìsì Year. Year end.

ɛ́ɛ̃ Yes.

ɛ́ɛ̃-ɛ̀ɛ̃ No.

ɛ́fà Name.

ɛ́fáà This thing. *(Used as substitute for a name of something that one cannot recall.*

ɛ́fífyá Grass, Weeds, Trash.

èfʉ́ghùfi A kind of mushroom that feels like a loaf of bread.

èg̃àr̃à Laziness.

èg̃ìg̃ó Denial.

ɛ́gɔ́rɔ́má Streaks, (usually water, or oil streaks left on utensils not washed properly).

ègbárà Medium-sized goat.

ègbàtà (1) Neighbour. as in: Ónyé ègbàtà úlwò *(neighbour)* (2) Boundary. as in: Ègbàtà ʼĺkporo

(Nkporo boundary).
(3) Average. Halfway.

ègbàtà-úzɔ̀ Cross roads. Junction.

ègbírìgbá Tiny snails.

ègbìsì Hair.

ɛ́gbɔ Vomit.

Ègbɔ́ji One of the three main communities of Ébíríbá comprising, Ame-ebya which divides into Ezi Elu, ʼĺdé Okorve. Ezi Ivíèrù, ʼĺdé Okẽfi, Ńdé Okórezi, and ʼĺdé Ichɔ̀ in Abya-Agbo; Amã-elu which divides into ʼĺdé Dike; Ńdé Ukõ, and Amã-agbɔ̀ which divides into Ńdé Mbila. Ńdé Ɛ́gwũ, ʼĺdé Ɔ́bya. ʼĺdé Ekpù, Ezi Agbɔ̀ also known as Amã-òbòsi.

ɛ́gbú Bond. Binding.

ègbʉ́ Tiny pieces.

ɛ́gbʉ̀ Gum - the fleshy tissue that covers the arches of the jaws and surrounds the necks of the teeth.

ègbùgbà Speak slanderously about an absent person.

ɛ́gbʉ́gbɔ̀ The skin, cover or outer coat of

fruits, yam, or
cassava

ègbừrừ Lineage.
Followers.

éghîrîghá Small pieces.

èghɔ́m Mishap. Mistake.

éghɔ́ri Nauseating
(smell, usually of
fish).

ègɔ́ Forgiveness. *Used
in,* Gbàá ègɔ́
(forgive).

ɛ́g̃u Open grassy land
with no trees.
Wilderness.

ɛ́g̃ú Hunger.

ègừ A refusal to run an
errand (applied
mostly to children).

ègwà Manners.
Behaviour. Design
patterns.

égwá A sense of loss;
Depression; Home
sickness; Nostalgia.

égwɔ̀ Cellulose strands
scraped off the
surface of raffia palm
fronds. It is used to
make dancing skirts
for some
masquerades.

égw̃ừ A god (said to
visit delinquents with
madness). A god of
madness. A male
name.

Ég̃wu-ènà One of the

age-grades in
Ébíríbá.

éñừ Fart; Gas or wind
passed through the
anus.

éñúñú A kind of ant.

éñwɔ́ Stomach. Belly.

éñwɔ́-íme Pregnancy.

éñwɔ́-òbíbí Stomach
ache.

éñwừ A kind of yam.

éñw̃úr̃ừ Sweat.
Perspiration.

èñwừrừ The eaves of a
thatch roof.

èñwùwñừrừ See
èhwừrừ

èñwừrừkpátá Measles.

ɛ̃̂ja Sand.

ɛ̃̂ja-m̀búrứ Sharp sand
from the river.

èjà Sacrifice. Divination.
ìcñu-: to sacrifice.
ìgba-: to divine.

ɛ̃̂jí Hair.

ɛ̃̂jí-àgbà: Beard.

ɛ̃̂jí-ímí Moustache.

éjú Head pad usually
made by folding
fabric into a circle.

éjú ŋdɔ Head pad made
of raffia palm fronds.

éjừ Dizzy.

éjú-ńdɔ Palmwine
tapster pad made of
raffia palm fronds.

èkà Tiny caterpiller
from an animal tick

that tends to burrow
into a human skin.

ɛ̃Ká Long. Tall. Height.

ɛ́ká Generic term for
the upper human
limb from the
shoulder to the finger
nails.

ɛ́ká-ɛ́mùmà Cheap. For
nothing.

ɛ́ká-ébe Witness.

ɛ́ká-íK̃e Miser.

ɛ́ká-j̀kpà Left handed.

ɛ́ká-m̀bj̀rj̀ Left hand.

ɛ́ká-mèrè Hand made;
(slang for) home-
made gin.

ɛ́kàng See **ɛ̃K̃ù.**

ɛ́ká-ɔ́fya Portion given
to anybody present
when something
(mostly a dead
animal) is found.

ɛ́ká-ɔ́K̃u Spendthrift.

ɛ́ká-ɔ́r̃u Occupation.
Handiwork.

ɛ́káràbwɔ̀ Two hands.
Thief. as in: Ɔ́ dè mé
ɛ́káràbwɔ̀ (*he is a
thief*).

ɛ̀kj̀kà (1) Termites. (2)
Marks. Patterns.

ɛ̃K̃ìK̃à-ébì Quills from a
Porcupine.

ɛ̀kj̀rj̀ Raches. Itchy skin
eruptions.

ɛ̀kj̀rj̀ká Dried thatch.

ɛ̀kj̀rj̀kɔ́ Tiny branches

of a cut big tree used
as firewood.

ɛ̀kj̀rj̀kɔ́rɔ Wiry strings
festooning mature
raffia palm trees.

ɛ̀kj̀rj̀-m̀bàn̄w̃úr̃ù Heat
rash.

ɛ̀kɔ́rɔ Period of dryness
after a long rainfall.

ɛ̀kɔ́rɔ Climbing plant
having one of the
tiniest leaves.

ɛ́kɔ̀m Malarial fever.

ɛ́kɔ̀m-ɛ́nyá-òd̃ò Yellow
fever. Hepatitis.

ɛ̀kɒà Bag. Sac. Pocket.

ɛ̀kɒà-ámù Scrotal sac.

ɛ̀kpà-átáng One of the
tradtional dance
followers of an Ìgwa-
máng celebrant
characterized by the
carrying of a
feathered contraption
on the back with a
giant bell.

ɛ̀kpàbúrùkòm Hoop
made of cane worn
by masquerades like
Mkpàrítùm to give
girt to their cloth-
skirt. (Efik
borrowing).

ɛ̀kpà-ég̃o See **ɛ̀kpá-
òkpòghò**

ɛ̀kpà-ímí-ókóghóró
Masquerade with a
sack costume and

grotesque face which accompanies the Òté-íríi traditional dance of the Ámógùdù community of Ébíríbá.

** èkpáluku** A kind of large land bird.

èkpá-ǹk̄úmà Bag of stone. Name of an age grade.

èkpà-ámu Scrotum (see **ámu**).

èkpà-mámiri Bladder.

èkpà-nwa Womb, Uterus.

èkpá-ŋvùrùmà Sack. Jute bag.

èkpá-òkpòghò Bag of money, formerly one hundred pounds, now two hundred naira.

èkpèbóng Stroke; Paralysis of some limbs of the body induced by Stroke. (Efik borrowing).

èkpékɔrɔ̀ Traditional masquerade of the Ukpo people usually festooned in climbing plant.

èkpétu Algae - any of various primitive chlorophyll-bearing plants widely distributed in fresh and salt water and moist lands, including the seaweeds and kelps.

èkpî Grime. Scum. (used to describe the yellowish-green plaque on the teeth of people with bad oral hygiene).

ékpîkpá Rash, usually one that covers a large portion of the body.

ékpîkpá-ńtà A small grey-colored animal that looks like the antelope.

ékpîkpá-íbù-óyi Goose pimples. A roughened condition of the skin in which its papillae are erected, caused by cold, shock, etc.,

èkpìrì Bedbugs. (chinch).

èkpìrì-ídò Golden brown (tailor) ants found mostly on Mango trees.

ékpù Knot. Irregular swelling

ékpù-ékà The tiny bone projection on the wrist. (Also, idiom for family)

ékpúghú Very tiny biting insect.

ɛ́kpúghútá-ɛ́kpųghųta (Of skin) Full of bumps and lumps.

ɛ́kpų-ìtìlì-ɛ́nyà The term is used to describe a situation when you thought you saw something but did not see anything.

ɛ́kpù-ǹkɔ́lɔ̀ Adam's apple.

ɛ́kpųkwàrà Phlegm - the stringy mucus secretion from the air passages usually discharged through the mouth.

ɛ́kpúkpú Lumps, as in: -ų́tàr̃à: lumps from cassava not pounded evenly.

ɛ́kpừrừkpừ A swelling. A protuberance on a part of the body.

ɛ́k̃ų́ Pubic hair (used mostly to describe those of females.

ɛ̀k̃ừ Wealth. Riches. Assets.

ɛ́k̃ù Fabric.

ɛ́k̃ù Traditional all-male secret society also called ɛ́kàng featuring the ừfỹè and comes out mostly at night.

ɛ̀kừbá Plant producing vegetable leaves and a stigma that itches.

ɛ́k̃ừk̃ừ Side.

ɛ̀kừkú Slang expression.

ɛ́k̃ừk̃ų́r̃ų Burnt or dried scrapping.

ɛ́k̃ừk̃ų́r̃ų-ími Dried phlegm scraped from the nose.

ɛ́k̃ừk̃ų́r̃ų-ńdi Burnt yam scrappings.

ɛ́k̃úpá Scales of dried grime and dirt.

ɛ́k̃ừ-údè A kind of broad leaves with a smooth surface found mostly in swamps, used in wrapping èsừsų́.

ɛ́kw̃á Cry.

ɛ̀kw̃á Egg.

ɛ̀kwà Event. Occasion.

ɛ̀kwàmini Towel.

ɛ̀kwásí Accessories. That which goes with.

ɛ́kw̃ú Cloth-eating moth.

ɛ́kwų́ Palm fruit.

ɛ̀kwų́ Nest.

ɛ̀kwừ Tangled up mesh of climbing plant and brush in the forest.

ɛ́kw̃ừ New growth on a yam tuber that had been cut while still in the soil.

ɛ́kwų́kwɔ́ Book. Paper. Leaf.

ɛ́kwų́kwɔ́-ɛ̀sùsú Broad

leaves used in
wrapping èsùsú.
Also used as slang
name for
international
passports.

ɛkwúkwɔ́-ìwá Cassava
leaves.

ɛkwúkwɔ́-ńɖù 'Book of
life', used as slang
name for the
American alien
registration card
(*Green card*).

ɛkwúkwɔ́-óťi *(Telfairia
occidentalis)* is a
tropical vine used as
a leaf vegetable and
for its edible seeds.
Also called Fluted
gourd, Fluted
pumpkin, or ụ́g̣u, the
young shoots and
leaves of the plant
are the main
ingredients of a
vegetable gumbo.
The large dark-red
seed can be eaten
boiled or roasted.

ɛkwúkwɔ́-òpòtóró
Broad leaves.

ɛkwúkwù̀ Epilepsy.

ɛ́ḷ̣ighịlị Too long a time.
Taking too much
time.

ɛ́ḷ̣ighịlị Tough, as in
under cooked meat.

ɛ́lù̀ghúlú Trash. Junk.

ɛ́lụ́lɔ́ The placenta and
foetal membranes
expelled from the
uterus after childbirth.

ɛ́lụ́lɔ́-ɔ́nu Spittle,
usually involuntary,
dripping from a
sleeping person's
mouth.

ɛ̀lwà Sickness. Malady.
Ailment.

ɛ́lyá Modern; Present
day.

ɛ̀'m̀bú At first. Before.

ɛ̀'m̀fé Simply

ɛ̀múmà For nothing.
With nothing.
Without anything.

Ɛ̀nàchíòkén The present
title of the paramount
ruler (the Ézè) of
Ɛ́bịrịbá.

ɛ̀'ńmécħi In conlusion.

ɛ̀nɔ́ Four.

ɛ́ŋu Bee. **mánú-:**
honey.

ɛ̀nù̀nù̀ A kind of tree, its
wood which burns
when fresh. (Efik
borrowing).

ɛ́nwụ́ntà Mosquito.

ɛ́nwù̀rù̀ Tobacco, Snuff.
ɛkwúkwɔ́-: tobacco
leaves.

ɛ́nwù̀rɔ́ku Smoke.

ɛ́nyá (1) Eyes. (2) Far.

ɛ́nyá-bèkéè: Eyeglasses;

Spectacles.

ɛ́nyá-ɛ́jʋ̀: Dizziness.

ɛ́nyá-ɛ́ƙá: 'Big eyed', greedv.

ɛ́nyá-ɛ̀nyà Far off. Afar.

ɛ́nyá-íke Boldness.

ɛ́nyá-kwá *Used to express:* "long time no see."

ɛ́nyá-míní-ɛkw̃á Tears.

ɛ́nya-mgbélú-óko Cock-eved.

ɛ́nyámkpɔ́ Blindness.

ɛ́nyá-ḿpághátá Cross-eved.

ɛ́nyá-ŋ́kíta Sty; Inflammation of the eyelid causing tiny boils around the roots of evelashes.

ɛ́nyá-ŋ́shi Conjuctivitis (also called pink eye); crusts that form on the eyelid overnight.

ɛ́nyá-nwámbá: Eyes with large pupils making them look like those of cats.

ɛ́nyá-nwéɡo: Eye with silver iris making it look like a coin.

ɛ́nyá르ɔ́ƙu Fireside, usually by the cooking place.

ɛ́nyá-òɗò Yellow eyes.

ɛ́nyá-úɗò With the right sense; without coercion.

ɛ́nyá-ʋ́ñwú Envious; jealous.

ɛ́nyáya Exactly. To the point. Perfect. Bull's eye.

ɛ̀nyìm Ocean. Sea.

ɛ́nyʋ́ Round squash fruit. Melon.

ɛ́nyʋ́nƙu Ax

ɛ́nyʋ́nyʋ-ŋ́gwɔ̀ Gelatinous sap of a cut palm tree.

ɛ̀ᵭá Branch (of a tree).

ɛ̀pʋ́ Pouting word used to dare or trivialize somebodv's boasting or threat, as in **ɛ̀pʋ́ kwá** *(I dare you).*

ɛ̀pʋ́rɛ̀pʋ́ Tickle, especially under the arm.

ɛ́rá Madness. Crazy.

ɛ́r̃á Breasts - the mammary glands. **míni-:** milk.

ɛ́r̃á-ɛ́ᵬù Excess flesh sticking out of a woman's armpit.

ɛ́r̃á-m̀gbɔ̀nɡbɔ̀: See **m̀gbɔ̀ŋgbɔ̀.**

ɛ́rá-ŋ́kĩ̀ta rabies; madness caused by rabid dog bite.

ɛ́r̃á-ŋ́kĩ̀ta dog's udder; items dangling in the manner of a dog's udder

ɛ́r̃á-nwántà A kind of

fruit that leaves a lingering sugar taste in the mouth long after it was eaten.

èríghítí Small species of lizard.

èrírí-ụ́zɔ̀ Track road. Footpath.

ɛ́rírí-ɛ́k̃á Parasitic round worm found in the intestines of man.

ɛ́r̃ú Bite.

Ɛ́r̃ụ̀ Short name of Ɛ́r̃ụ̀chúkú (Arochukwu).

èrùghérù Mischievous.

ɛ́r̃únsị Fetish. Statue. Image. Idol. A male name.

ɛ́r̃únsị-ápĩ̀r̃àpĩ́ Idol; Carved wooden image.

èsáà Seven

èsátɔ Eight.

èsátɔ-ńsèkátá: Kindergaten doodle using the figure eight.

èsụ̀ *Used in:* Ɔ́kpá èsụ̀ - a kind of foot disease that makes sufferers walk on tiptoes.

èsụ̀sụ́ A staple corn meal of the Ɛ́bị́rị́bá people made by boiling ground corn paste wrapped in leaves and eaten with vegetable soup.

ɛ̃́tá (Sorts of) wild plant with prickly leaves.

ètʃi Name for a child performing the traditional *ígba-ɲ́nùnù*.

ètʃili Dark.

ètɔ́ Three.

ɛ́tú Stick for cleaning teeth. Chewing stick.

ɛ́tù Comparison.

ɛ́tú ɛ́kɛ́rɛ̀ Guinea worm

ɛ́túrụ (Of a surface) smooth, wet, polished, etc., so that it is difficult to hold, to stand on, or to move on.

èwà Early, as in: Má èwà *(be early)*.

ɛ́wáká-ɔ́nu Scurvy; disease characterized by sore cuts at the corners of the mouth.

ɛ́wɔ́ Gray hair.

ɛ́wɔ̀ Toad.

ɛ́wɔ̀-pànya A kind of strong-smelling, strong tasting dried seasoning fish.

ɛ́wɔ́lí Long and narrow, woven thatch placed on the centre of a roof to act as ridge cover for the area where the two roofs meet.

èwɔ̀rɔ̀ Branches of a cut

tree.

ɛ̀wʋ̀ (1) Play. (2) Joke,

ɛ̀wʋ̀-áránK̃é Play likely
to cause injury.

ɛ̀wʋ̀rʋ́-mang
Frightening chill.

ɛ̀zà Want, Covet, Crave,

as in: Íri-ɛ̀zà (*to
have a fondness or
passion for*).

ɛ́zízà Broom.

ɛ̀zʋ̀ghʋ̀zʋ̀ Dried tree
limbs and leaves in
cleared farmland.

f

fá A squeezing tightness, as in: Fá ŋfághá *(be tight - of clothing)*.

f̃á Yell.

fàá Squeeze, as in: Fàá òlígbù *(squeeze the chlorophyl out of the òlígbù leaves)*.

fáɓà Slot into.

fàkàa Soft and mushy.

fá-ŋfagha Close fitting

fàyí Stuff into; squeeze into, as in: Fàyí èkpà *(squeeze into a pocket)*.

fé (1) Sprinkle, as in: Fé mini *(sprinkle water)*. (2) Jump. Fly. **-ɓà:** jump into. **-ɗà:** jump down. **-ƙúr̃ú:** jump onto. **-lyè:** jump up. **-pù:** fly off. (3) Wave, as in: Fé èkà *(wave the hands)*. Fé ùfùfé *(of wind blowing)*.

féfù Name for "Faith" - First Century Gospel Church.

fìfĩì Quick outing.

fífỹe Wave vigorously.

fípù Edge out.

fìyí Wedge.

f̃ó Parade.

f̃ókpùú Mention constantly.

fɔrú Marry (a woman who had been divorced, widowed or had a child out of wedlock).

f̃ùtá Meet. See each other.

f̃ùú See.

f̃ùú-ɛnyá Love.

fyárárá Slide.

fyàtú (1) To spit into the palm of the hand as a lubricant while using a hoe or matchet.

fyé Bind (with a rope), as in: Fyé ŋƙu *(tie up a bundle of firewood)*. (2) Grab (in a bear hug).

fỹé Wipe (with the finger), as in: Fỹé ɛ̃w̃úr̃ù.

f̃ṽèé Whip.

fyɔ́ɔ́ Make a hole. Open by drilling, as in: Fyɔ́ɔ́ mànyì *(uncork a wine bottle)*. Fyɔ́ɔ́ ŋtúbe *(drill a hole)*.

fyɔ́-ŋfyɔ́ghɔ́rɔ́ Narrow and tight (space).

fyɔ́rɔ́rɔ́ (1) Whistle.

g

g̃á Scratch. as in: G̃á
ḿbwɔ̀ *(scratch with
finger nails).*

gàá Go. Move.

gágha Pass.

gàghásá Come by.

gághàsá Come over (to
this side).

g̃ághá-g̃ághá A low
wooden half-gate at the
door of a traditional
kitchen to keep
domestic animals out or
in.

gàñé Go on your way.

gàní Bye. Go.

gàví Thread.

g̃áñá-g̃áñá Quick and
lively.

gàrí Meal made out of
grated, dried and fried
cassava.

g̃é Go on. Keep moving.
String.

g̃èbé Spread. as in: G̃èbé
ánwu *(spread in the
sun).*

g̃èbé-ŋ́cñì Listen *(spread
ears).*

g̃èchỹé String across.

gédé (Of a person)
Scrawny.

gédégèdè Behave
awkwardly.

gérégéré Light

consistency (of soup,
cream, etc).

gídígìdì Disorder.

gídígìdìgídí Commotion.
Stampede. Disorder.

g̃òɗò (Of a house, arena,
or market place) Quiet
and empty of people.

g̃óó Buy. (used mostly in):
-úgbɔ̀ghɔ̀: buy
vegetables. **-àlì:** buy
land.

gɔ̀ɔ́ Deny, as in: Ịgɔ-ègìgɔ́
(to deny).

gɔ̀zyé Bless.

g̃ù Yearn for. (be hungry
for).

g̃ú (1) Read. as in: Ịg̃u-
ɛ́kwúwkɔ́ *(to read a
book).* (2) Count. (3)
Figure. (4) Sing.

g̃ú-ɗà: Read through.
Count, as in: Ịg̃ù ɔg̃u
(to count numbers).

gúgò Be sensitive, as in:
Gúgò éze *(set the teeth
on edge).*

g̃ùkátá Add up.

g̃ú-kɔ́tá: Calculate.

g̃ú-nyi: Count in (add).

g̃úpù: Count out (subtract).

gùú (1) Dig, as in: Ígu ŋ́dí
(to dig up yam). (2)
Stab. Jab.

gùú (1) Drip, as in: Gùú-

pàá *(dripping all over).*
(2) Refuse to (help out
or run an errand. (3)
Name, as in: Ígù̱-ɛ́fà

(to give a name).
g̃ù̱z̄ó Stand.
g̃ù̱z̄ó-ɔ́tɔ Stand (upright).

gb

gbà Happen.

gbá-ùrị̀ghì Deceive in an attempt to dodge.

gbàá (1) Shoot. (2) Ride. (3) Sting. (4) Write. (5) Buy (hoe, matchet). (6) Roast (corn).

gbàá-ẹ̀jà Divine, or engage in divination.

gbàá-mànù Produce oil.

gbàá-menyi Bleed, or produce blood.

gbàá- ḿkpị̀ Be paired, or come in pairs.

gbàá-ḿpa Be stuck; be perplexed, or in a bind.

gbàá-ónyà Set a trap.

gbàá-ókpúkpú Set fractured bones.

gbáɓà Run into.

gbàbá Take heart, or be comforted.

 gbàbá Set (a trap).

gbàchỹé Lock up, or bolt (a door).

gbà-ɛ̀kà Empty handed.

gbàá-ɛ́ká Hurry up.

gbágbalì A kind of twining, climbing plant.

gbàgbùrù-gbúrù (1) Surround; (2) run in circles, or around

gbàgbwó Shoot to kill.

gbághàá Overtake. Cross over. Go over.

gbàghà-gbàghà Large and wide.

gbàgháryá Turn around.

gbàghásá Run by (some place)

gbàghébé Leave open or agape.

gbàg̃ó Walk on (a fallen tree or log).

ghágwò jú ɛ́nyà Confuse, or be confusing.

gbáɦwùɦú Run away and get lost.

gbàjwó (Of liquid) fill to the brim.

gbàjyé Break (a rigid object.

gbàK̃úr̃ú Run up.

gbàkw̃únyí Run to join, or catch up with (someone).

gbàkw̃úr̃ú Run up to

gbàkwúr̃ú Be stumped; be baffled.

gbánwò Change.

gbànywá Turn off (lamp or light).

gbályá Try hard; make an attempt, or effort.

gbàpụ̀ụ́ Separate liquid from solid, or another liquid.

gbàpwó Open (especially

locks, or doors).

gbàrɛ̀kà See **gbà-ɛ̀ká.**

gbáryá Dissolve; sieve (dried grated cassava).

gbásá Concerning; About.

gbásàá Spread. Scatter.

gbàtáñú Escape; Run away.

gbàtú Write down.

gbàyí (1) Pour in. (2) Write.

gbàyí Mischievous act of urging somebody to do something destructive or wrong.

gbáẑèñí Dissolve. Melt.

gbàẑínyí Loan, or lend (to someone).

gbàẑírí Borrow.

gbàẑúñú Stand.

gbàẑúñú-ɔ́tɔ́ Stand up.

gbázwàá Crush with the feet.

gbázwòó Run together (of people) to form a crowd.

gbèé (1) Crawl, as in: Gbèé ígbe *(crawl on hands and knees)* like

babies. (2) Bent. Crooked.

gbéghàtá Be bent and twisted.

gbémà-gbémà (In boxing, or fighting) punch all over.

gbéŋ Sound of the punch (in a fight).

gbéŋ-gbéŋ Throbbing (headache).

gbígbírírí Crudely thick.

gbípá Crudely thick and heavy.

gbɔ̀ɔ́ (1) Vomit. (2) Bark (of a dog). (3) Pare (trees). (4) (Of water) boil.

gbòchwó Halt. Stop.

gbòó Stop, as in: Gbòó ɔ̀g̃ù *(stop fighters).*

gbɔ̀tɔ́ Drop; put down.

gbùpwó Clear, or create an opening.

gbùrùgbúrù Around. Round. Circle.

gbùú Cut.

gbúpù Spit out.

gbwòó Kill

gh

ghá Turn.

ghàá Leave without. Abandon, as in: Ụ́gbɔ́ ghà yá (the vehicle left without him).

ghághà (Of a Person) difficult to deal with.

ghághàghá In a disorderly fashion.

ghàghárvá Turn around.

ghàkɔ́ Save the situation; crisis control.

ghárá-ghàrà-ghárá Confused state.

gháṛìpú Take off, as in: Gháṛìpú ɔ́sɔ *(run off suddenly).*

ghá-ụ̀bị̀bàrí Twist.

ghàyí (1) Lie, as in: Ghàyí ụ́gha (tell a lie). (2) Sprinkle. as in: Ghàyí ŋ́nú (sprinkle in some salt).

ghèé (1) Fry, as in: Ghèé ánu (frv meat). (2)

ghɔ́rɔ̀-ghɔ́rɔ̀ Activity. Noise indicating a disturbance of the peace.

ghɔ́rụ́ Harvest, or pluck (fruits).

Open, as in: Ghèé úghere (open the mouth for a yawn). (3) Cook till well done. (4) Cut (as with a knife).

ghèé-úghere Yawn.

ghém-ghèm Act of greed; being unsatisfied.

ghétá-ghètà Feeling of being unsatisfied (after eating).

ghí Your, as in: Ɛ́ká ghi (your hand).

ghóró-ghòrò Discomfort.

ghóró-ghòrò-ghóró Uncomfortable feeling of general malaise.

ghɔ́ Go wrong; Be fouled up.

ghɔ̀gbwó Deceive, cheat or scam (a person).

ghɔ̀ɔ́ (1) Catch. Pick. (2) To trick, or cheat. (3) Change into, or develop.

ghɔ̀sá Understand. Comprehend.

ghụ́màá Make noisy outbursts. Complain loudly.

gw

gwàá (1) Mix. as in: Gwàá yá ágwá *(mix it up)*. (2) Appease, as in: Gwá mang *(appease the gods)*.

gwóɓà Take inside.

gwóɓàsá Bring in, or introduce

gwòbúrú Take some.

gwógwo See **gwòghórógwò**

gwòghórógwò Traditional dance known for its destructive behaviour.

gwòó 1. Grind. 2. Take a picture. 3. Draw, Illustrate.

gwópù Take away.

gwòrú Take.

gwòrúchágbwó Take all.

gwòsá Bring.

gwòba Twist (cloth into a head pad).

gwɔ́ɔ́ Heal . Cure. as in. Gwɔ́ɔ́ èlwà *(cure a malady)*. Concoct, as in: Gwɔ́ɔ́ ɔ́gw̃ù *(prepare a medicinal concoction)*. Also, Gwɔ́ɔ́ ɔ̀kážu *(prepare ɔ̀kážu salad]* which involves mixing various ingredients.

gwɔ́ɔ́-úr̃a Snore.

gwɔ̀ɒì Dirtily wet.

gwɔ̀yí Turn a corner.

gwú Finish.

gwú Swim.

gw̃ùh̃á Wipe away or clean (faeces).

gw̃ùú (1) Wrap, as in Gw̃ùú ŋgw̃ùgw̃ù *(wrap up a parcel)*. (2) Be humbled or taken aback (by an unexpected news or action).

ɦ

ɦà   Will (used as an auxiliary to indicate future action). *ányi ɦà àbyá* (we will come).

ɦàá   (1) Be enough. (2) Conjure up; as in *ɦàá-mini* (make rain).

ɦábà   Scoop into.

ɦábá   Be enough

ɦá-ɛ́nừ   Make a sound (usually to answer).

ɦànyí   Scoop in.

ɦápừú   Scoop out.

ɦàtá   Be equal.

ɦèé   (1) Deflate. Become smaller, as in Ɦèé ɛ́ɦwɔ *(hold in the stomach)*. (2) Dodge. Sneak.

Pilfer.

ɦèghè-ɦèghè   Wobbly. Shaky.

ɦépừừ   Sneak off.

ɦèt́áɦí   Abscond. Sneak away.

ɦừbá-áma   Make special note; To note well

ɦừú   (1) Burn. (2) Reject.

ɦừú-áɦừ   (Of a child) rejecting or refusing to eat certain food items.

ɦừú-ɔ́nu   Set a price.

ɦừtá   Roast and eat.

ɦw̃àá   Roast or broil (especially on an open fire).

ĥ

ĥàá   Let go, as in: Hàá
  va *(let go of him)*.

ĥápụ̀ụ́   Leave, as in:
  Hápụ̀'m éká *(leave
  me alone)*.

ĥèé   Lift (a spread mat
  or flat object).

ĥépụ̀ụ́   Lift off.
  Remove. (Used to
  describe the removal
  of a spread carpet,
  mat or cloth, as in:
  Hépụ̀ụ́ úté *(remove
  the mat)*.

ĥɔ́pụ̀sá   Pick out; select.

ĥɔ́ɔ́   Make a selection;
  choose.

ĥɔ̀rú   Pick out; Choose
  for self.

ĥwòó   Wipe

ĥwòó   Be lost. Get lost.

ĥwɔ̀K̃éṝí   Yank off (a
  large piece).

ĥwɔ́twòó   Lift up and
  put down (of a
  cooking pot).

ĥwɔ̀ɔ́   (1) Remain, as in:

Ɔ́ ĥwɔ̀ èbwɔ́ɔ *(there
  are two remaining)*.

ĥwɔ̀pụ̀   Lift off (a
  cooking pot).

ĥwụ́   Body.

ĥwụ̀bá   Enfold.

ĥw̃ùĥú   Be lost.

ĥwụ́-ítaĥiK̃e   Of good
  health. Healthy.

ĥwụ́-ɔ́K̃u   Hot body.
  Restlessness.

ĥwụ́-nyụ́á   Blow out the
  flame (of a fire, lamp,
  or lantern).

ĥwúpụ̀ú   Erase.

ĥwụ̀pụ̀ụ́   Blow off.

ĥwụ̀rí   Converse.

ĥw̃ùú   Form a welt.

ĥwụ̀ụ́   Tell (a story).
  Blow (air).

ĥwùú   (1) Bend (down).
  (2) Rub. (3) Loss.

ĥwụ̀ụ́-ụ̀ĥwụ́   Hurting;
  Give or cause pain;
  ache.

I

í- *Used as infinitive marker:* To, as in: I:'lwo *(to swallow).*

í In, At, as in: Í'mí *(in the nose).*

íbé (1) Part, as in: Íbé ŋdi *(piece of yam).* (2) Place, as in: Íbé ányi *(our place).* (3) Since, as in: Íbé ịbyà *(since you came).*

íbè Companion. Relative, as in: Íkwú r'íbè *(relatives and extended family).*

íbe Surety, or mortgage (Used in) Ịgbaba-íbe *(to place as collateral).*

íbé-ɛ́nyà Far place. Distant.

íbéghéré Piece.

íbé-máng-wɔ̀-íyi A valley without a stream said to have been denied it of that privilege by the spirits.

ìbèríbè Stupid, as in Ónyé ìbèríbè *(stupid person).*

íbé-ɔ́rị̀ There. Overthere.

íbì Hydrocele. Enlarged scrotum, also called Elephantiasis Scroti

íbì Waste, or Loss, used in *lá-íbì* (go to waste).

íbí *Used in:* Íbí ɛ́kwa to describe a person who cries a lot; a cry baby.

ìbìrìbè Large ash particles.

íbìrì-óbìrì Children's imaginary cooking play.

íbiri-ɔ́ƙu Get fire, as in hot coal for use in starting another fire.

ìɓó Inside the branches of a Palm tree.

íɓóříɓó A tiny piece.

íbù (1) Fat. Obese. (2) To cut or nip the tip, as in: Íbù úgw̃ù *(to circumcise).*

íbú Load. Baggage. Burden. Cargo.

íbu-mànyì Traditional marriage ceremony in which the groom and his family present drinks to the bride's family.

íbu-mànyì-ŋ́jụrụ Literally, "question drink;" it refers to drink presented to a

bride's father as a
preliminary to a
bethrotal.

íbù-óyi A sensation of
cold, often with
shivering.

íbúrúsɔ̀ Infant ailment
characterized by the
exhibition of
symptoms of being
scared.

íbu-úlwò The act in
which the bride's
family gives her gifts
(mostly kitchen
utensils) to take to
her new home.

ìbyé A kind of plant
producing hairy pods
which irritate the
skin and make the
victims scratch.

ìbye To cut in tiny slices
(onions, leaves, okra
etc.

ìɓye-ɔmá To give a hug.

íchèmbè To depend.

íchéku A tree which
produces the velvet
tamarind with a stem
that makes a good
firewood when dry.

ìchínyòm Old woman.

ìchi Tattoo, scarification,
or facial marks.

ìchíta Grass.

íchìtà To crack and eat
(kernel nuts).

ìchì-údè Traditional
palm wine tapper

íchò̃ Different. Separate.

í ìch̃yè In the olden days.

ìch̃yoƙè Old man.

ídònyí Flood or torrent
caused by rainfall.

ídìdè (1) Earth worm. (2)
Athlete's foot.

ídò See **ɛ̀kpịrị̀-ídò.**

ídònyi Water that has
overflowed from a
source such as a river
onto a previously dry
area.

ídula-nwágbɔghɔ̀ To
give out (a girl) in
marriage.

ídu-ŋ́dí Tending yam
tendrils.

ĩ́fé Thing. Something.

ĩ́fè Light. Civilization.

ĩ́fé-alulwà "That which
softens." Used to
describe mostly food
items that
complement (softens)
other food items. eg.
The role of butter on
bread, or okra on
vegetable.

ĩ́fé-ɛ́fĩ́fyá Trash
container.

ĩ́fé-ɛ̀múmà Nonsense.
Useless.

ĩ̌félè See **ĩ̌félèmantà**

ífélèmantà Something,
(used as substitute

for a name of
something that one
cannot recall).

ífénsɔ Forbidden thing.
Abomination.

ífé-ńchìì Ear-ring.

ífé-ŋdòři Sauce. Soup.

ífé- ófo Soup-making
ingredients like meat,
fish, crayfish, etc.

ífé-ólù Necklace.

ífé-ɔjɔɔ Bad thing. Evil.

ífé-ónwón (Something,
or act) not readily
describable.

íféře Shame. Shyness.
Reserved.

ífì Revenge.

ífìfé Madness. Insanity.

ífo Roam, or move back
and forth.

ìgbé Box.

ígbe (Of a toddler) crawl
on hands and knees.

ìgbé-óžù Casket. Coffin.

ígbèghìrì A steel tool
with a rough, ridged
surface for
sharpening a knive,
matchet or hoe. A
file.

ìgbí Illiterate.

ígbìjí Heavy.

ìgbìjì A kind of trap in
which stones and dirt
are piled on an
angled frame-work.
Any animal that goes

under it to set it off is
crushed.

Ìgbò The Igbo people -
their language.

ígbubù To cut.

ìgbùdù Plenty. A lot.

ìgbu-agha The first
achievement of a
young man. A form
of making your 'first
bone,' characterized
by the killing of a
bird by a pre-teen
boy.

ìgbu-efĩ To sacrifice a
bullock usually for
burial purposes.

ìgbúgbú Meal cooked
and eaten with not
enough ingredients.

ígbúji-ŋgwɔ To bore a
hole in a raffia palm
tree shoot to extract
the wine sap.

ígburi-ɛwù To play. To
display (a dance).

ìgìrì Nuisance; Trouble.
Scare.

ígù Palm tree branch.

ígu-ŋdi Complete
harvesting of yam.

ìgùm A kind of yam.

ìgùrùbè Locust.

ígwo (1) Heaven. Sky.
(2) To grind (corn).

ígwò Iron. Bicycle.
Any mechanical
contraption.

ígwú Louse.

ígwú-ɔK̀àr̃à Body louse
found in items of
clothing.

ígw̃u-máng To place on
oath.

íɦ̃wù To be lost.

Íɦ̃ébu One of the
subdivisions of
Ám̃éK̃e in Ɛ́bír̃íbá
comprising Ńdé
Okórezi. Ńdé
Okétĕke, Ńdé
Ɔnúégbè, Ńdé ÁK̃a,
Ɉ́dé Ɔbyà. Ńdé
Oryentà. Ɉ́dé Omóji,
and Ɉ́dé Irónkwà.

ìɦ̃í Reason, as in *n'ìɦ̃í*
Because.

íɦ̃wɔpù-ekwũ Literally
'to remove a hearth'
Divorce.

íɦ̃wú Face. Front.
Ahead.

íɦ̃wú-ɛtɔ Sixty.

íɦ̃wùɦ̃ù To disappear.
To get lost.

íɦ̃wú-máng Shrine.

Íɦ̃w̃úngw̃ù One of the
subdivisions of
Ám̃éK̃e in Ɛ́bír̃íbá
comprising íɦ̃w̃úezi.
Ɉ́dé óɦ̃wúɔnu, Ɉ́dé
Okóró-Ɉ́ta, and Ɉ́dé
Ɔnwúka.

íɦ̃wú-ĩʃo One hundred.

íɦ̃wú-kpékpéré
Straight forward.

íɦ̃w̃ú-ŋmà Edge of a
knife.

iɦ̃w̃ú-ɔ́jɔ́ɔ Bad luck.
Misfortune.

íɦ̃wú-ɔ́kɒà Shin.

íɦ̃w̃ú-ɔ́má Good luck.

íɦ̃w̃úr'àbwɔ̀ (1) Double
face. Falseness.
Hyprocrite. (2)
Forty.

íɦ̃w̃úr̃'àz̃ú Front and
back (used to
describe fabric with
no wrong side.

íɦ̃wùr̃ì To converse.

íɦ̃w̃úr̃'ìɦ̃w̃ú Face to face.

íɦ̃w̃ú-úzɔ̀-ígwò Main
road.

ĩ̀jè Journey. Walk.

ĩ̀jè-ág̃u Tiger's walk.
Graceful. Female
name

íjéghíjé Water beads
and droplets
appearing on the skin
after a bath.

ĩ̀je-ŋ́nɔ A disorder of
the intestine marked
by abnormally
frequent and fluid
evacuation of the
bowels.

ĩ̀jè-ɔ́má Farewell. To
have a nice journey.

ìjóghó Ornamental
ringlets worn on
ankles mostly by
maidens yet to be

engaged for marriage.

ñji House fly.

íjí Dew.

íjijè To mock. Mimicry.

ìjì-ólù Neck (back of the head).

íƙé Strength. Power. Authority.

íƙè Bottom. Anus. Rectum. Buttocks.

íƙebe-èkpà (Literally) packing the luggage of one about to embark on a journey.

íƙèñèr̃è-ŋ̃si Left over faeces (in the anus).

íƙé-ishi To plait the hair.

íƙékwó Perhaps.

íke-ŋ́dí A process whereby a growing yam tuber is cut off while still underground such that the left over portion regrows.

íƙéñgà Household god.

íƙé-ɔ̀gwụgwụ Tiredness. Exhaustion.

íƙé-okwu (1) (Slang for) drinking cup.; (2) ability to speak.

ìkéré Dye producing leaves used for polishing mud floors to a shine.

íkésu Sap.

ìkètá Not ripe (of fruit).

ìƙíƙé Powerful. Strong. Hard.

ìƙíƙé-ágbóru Display of boldness usually to one's detriment.

íkìkére-éze The grinding the teeth. Gnash.

ìkìrì A small tailless animal found on trees. Also called -ɛ́károbù: because it holds its upper limbs to its chest.

íkíríbyá Cowry shell.

íkìrìkè-ŋ́jílá Snail shells.

ìkìtì-ɔ́kpà Foot steps.

ìkó Cup. Drinking vessel.

ìƙó Friend (usually of the opposite sex in an extramarital romantic relationship).

ìkó-àgbɔ̀ Cup made out of a gourd; large cup made from calabash.

íƙókwu (1) Another name for cup. (2) Ability to speak.

ìƙóm Male.

íkòrò A giant, hollowed-out wooden, talking drum used to relay messages to far distance and played by beating the edges of the hollow with fists.

ìkóró'gbòlóko An effeminate boy or man.

íkpe Judgment.

íkpé-èkpérè To pray.

ìkpèghè (1) Money. (2) Female. (3) Derogatory term for a lover of meat.

íkpèrè Knee.

íkpèré-ŋkɔgbé K-leg or knocked knee.

íkperi-chi Worship of a deity. Pray.

íkpíkpé An ironical or scornful utterance contemptuous and taunting language.

ìkpìrìkpè Animal skin drums.

ìkpìrìkpé-ɔ̃g̃ù 'War drums'. War dance.

ìkpó Wooden bells worn by hunting dogs to chase animals towards the armed hunters.

ìkpóò Non-initiate (of a masquerade group, or a similar traditional secret society).

íkpù (1) To cover self (with hat or covering). (2) Female genital.

ìkpú An undeveloped stem, branch, or shoot of a plant, with runimenary leaves or unexpanded flowers, as in budding okra and mushroom.

ìkpù Conference. Conspiracy. Tete-a-tete.

íkpú If you crawl (through a hole).

íkpu-ɔgbù A kind of mushroom.

ìkpúrikpú Maggot.

ìkúbe A kind of gray-coloured anthill that looks like it is wearing a hat.

ìkù-ɛnyà Eye lashes. Eye brow.

ìkù-nwántà-úzù To take in an apprentice.

íkw̃ò Mortar.

íkw̃o To be erect and stiff (of penis).

íkwo To agree.

íkwoR̃er̃i To yank off (usually a head).

íkwú Extended matrilineal family.

íkwu (1) To speak (a language). (2) To buy (salt).

ìkw̃ù Language that is coarse or bad aimed at somebody.

íkwúghú Door or window frame.

íkw̃úkw̃úmá Council members of the traditional ruler's court.

íkwú-nna The paternal family.

íkwú-nne The maternal family.

íle-àli Farm land surveying.

ìlèghè Like. As.

íle-ɔ̀mɔ́ghɔ̀ (Of grandmothers) helping their daughters as they nurse their own babies.

ílì (1) Grave. (2) To bury.

ílí (Used in) *ígbu ílí* to give (someone) a beating.

ìlèghè As. Like.

ílu (1) Story. Proverb. Adage. (2) To buy (drinks).

ílú Bitter.

ílù (1) A sum (of money) that somebody is ordered to pay for breaking a law or rule. (2) To make a mistake, or error.

ílùghúlú Vulgar. Naughty. Voyeur.

ímařìfè To be knowledgeable.

íme Pregnancy. Inside. Among.

ímebezi To correct. To repair.

ímechĩ To close. To conclude.

íméji Liver.

ímela "You've done it" – Greeting of appreciation for a gift, or services rendered.

ímenyi-ìfè Gift giving to a bride prior to wedding.

ímérí (Of a wrong)unavenged.

imes̃jɦa To clean.

ímí (1) Nose. (2) The slimy mucous secretion from the nose.

ímí mpya Deformed nose.

ímí-ómúmé Catarrh; infection of the nose; flu.

ìmúmù Deaf-mute. (Efik borrowing).

ímùrì To share something (usually) small.

ímúřímú Tiny (in size).

ìnìnì-ógw̃u A kind of wild, green vegetable leaves with tiny thorns on the stem.

ìnùmàřà Plenty.

ìnyímɔ̀ka Supreme leadership and

adjudicating body of the Ébiriba people comprising mostly persons who have performed the traditional Igwa-mang ceremony.

ínyìrì Dirt. Charcoal.

ípo To peel or remove the skin or shell.

ípòghìrì The skin (of fish).

ípòghòrò Thorn from a dried palm frond base.

ìpòtò Wide fencing material made of thatch. (Efik borrowing).

íré Tongue.

ìrè Potent. Efficacious, as in: Ɔ́gwǜ'a dị̀ ìrè *(this medicine is efficacious).*

íre To sell.

írér'àbwɔ̀ "Two tongues'. Liar.

íré-ún̄wù A kind of ailment in which the tongue is so sore that eating becomes a nightmare. Scurvy

ìrí Ten.

írí Music. Dance.

íri-ágbá (of skin disease) to spread all over..

írí-ághà Traditional war dance.

ìrí-èbwɔ́ɔ Twelve.

ìrí-ènɔ́ Fourteen.

ìri-èsáa Seventeen.

ìrí-èsátɔ Eighteen.

ìrí-ètɔ́ Thirteen.

ìrí-ètólu Nineteen.

íríghírí Loose pieces.

ìrí-ĩ́ší Sixteen.

ìrí-ĩ̃šó Fifteen.

íri-ŋ̀chà (Of cloth) worn thin.

író To be in enmity. Hatred.

írù-įkpɔ̀ghɔ́ To flirt with.

ìr̃ú-ɔ̃k̄àr̃à A married woman.

ìrúrú New growths of weeds in a farm.

íshí Head.

ĩ̃shi Smell.

ìshì Blindness.

íshí-ákịká Dawn; Early in the morning.

íshí-ɛ́kpĩ̂kpá Scalp disease characterized by tiny pustules.

íshí-ɛ́wɔ Gray hair.

íshí-ikik̃e Stubborn, (strong head).

ìshíshì (Corn) cob.

ìsìsìboloyi Earthworm

ìsìm One of the masquerades of the Ébịrịbá-Ùmón dances with a long tail. Tail (Efik borrowing).

ìsìm-ísìm (Of punching with the fist or eating) in a disorderly fashion.

ísímokoto Green-surfaced lake in Ùkṗó.

ísí-ŋkwɔ́cħá Without hair on the head.

ísí-ɔ́jɔ́ɔ̀ Stubborn. Unamenable.

ísí-ɔ̀ƙàr̃à (1) Head tie. Scarf. (2) Edge of a wrap.

ísí-òkpòghò Business capital.

ísí-ókwu (1) Basis of a speech or conflict. (2) Talk.

ísí-ɔwụwa Head-ache.

ìsísì Exhausted corn cob.

ìsìsìboloyí Earthworm.

ísí-ụ̀tútụ̀ Early morning.

ísí-y'ɔ́dù The fact of the matter. Substance or meaning (usually of speech).

ĩsŏ Five.

ìsòngò See ŋ́táng ŋ̀kàndà

ìtè Pot.

ìtè-ígwò Iron pot.

ĩte-íkòrò To dance to the beat of the ikoro giant wooden slit drum

ĩte-írí To dance.

ìtè-ɔ́fa Pot hung on a palm tree to collect wine sap from a hole made in the shoot.

ítè-òtù Clay pot.

íte-ŋ̀zu Painting the body with clay chalk.

íte-úfyé Painting the body with red camwood.

íte-ùryè Painting the body with any form of coloring.

ìtì Novice. Beginner.

ìtìghítì (Defunct language of Ɔ̀gbụ̀ for) Night.

ìtìlì Darkness.

ítù Heap.

ítùm Farmland after new yams have been used up, usually soft and easy to till.

ítũri To divide and share out to participants.

Ítũri-ɛ̀kũ The distribution of property, usually those of a diseased person, among stake holders.

ítùtù Plenty.

íwèrè Dead tissue (mostly from snakes) sloughed off skin.

íwó anger.

íwòwò One of the dancers of an Ịgwa-

máng celebrant
characterized by a
skirt of tightly folded
cloths.

íwu (1) To build. (2)
To cook. (3) A kind
of three-leafed yam.

íwu-àkwũkwã To build
a bridge (usually a
communal effort).

ìwú Law.

íwu-usókwũ To build a
kitchen.

íyà Yes, (answer to a
question).

ìyáà Mother.

íye-ɔ̀k̃u Burning of bush
for farming purposes.

íyi Water springing from
a rock. Stream.

Spring.

ìzèmóò An expression
used to indicate 'Not
me'.

ízì (Something)
shockingly
frightening or scary.

íz̃ì To blow (through the
nose).

íz̃ì-ímí To blow the nose.

íz̃ì-ŋ́dừ̀ghú To sneeze.

ízizi Dried palm fronds
without the midriff
used as rope mostly
for tying èsừ̀sứ.

ìzù Meeting.

ízù To be complete.

ízù The day. **-t̃áà:** today.

ízù-ík̃é To rest.

ìzúmá Stupidity.

Ị̣

í- *Used as infinitive marker:* To, as in: I:'ta *(to chew)*.

ị̀ba To be rich (wealthy).

ị̀bá Shorts. Pants. Trousers.

ị̀bá A kind of limb-paralysing ailment.

ị̀ɓà (1) To be initiated (into a secret society). (2) To grab.

ị̀ɓà-ékpè Initiation into the ékpè society.

ị̀ɓà-ékpè-èsáa After initiation into the ékpè society, the acquisition of seven more quotas of ékpè which could be handed down to sons.

ị̀ɓà-ɛ̀g̃àr̃à To be boring. To feel lazy.

ị̀ɓà-ɛ̀kū Initiation into the eku secret society.

ị̀bàghàbúghú Excess. Too much.

ị̀bághálá Children disease characterized by the passing of a loose greenish or yellowish stool.

ị̀ɓami To grunt and groan.

ị̀ɓà-ɔ̀bɔ̀n Initiation into the traditional all male secret society.

ị̀bàrà The act of flaunting. To be showy.

ị̀bɔ̀ŋ State of disgust following the excessive eating of a particular food.

ị̀bu To be or become.

ị̀ɓụrɔ́mú Ceremony in which an age grade picks up palm fronds thrown by the enachioken—an act which signifies the recognition of the incoming age grade as having replaced the retired age grade.

ị̀chà Fishing in which a large basket, or hand-held netting basket is wedged at the narrow portion of a stream or river and then the river is stomped from the top to drive all the fish to the basket.

ị̀chà-íyi Dredging, usually of a small river to achieve depth.

ị̀chɔ To seek for.

ị̀chɔpụ̀sà To find. To discover.

ị̀chu To chase

ị̀chụ-áfà New year day celebration in which villagers throw sweepings in the street as form of chasing the old year away and ushering in the new vear.

îchuta To chase each other.

îchu̯-ntá Hunting.

îdi To be.

îdi-ŋma Beauty.

îdị-íK̃íK̃é Difficulty

îdɔba ókpókóró Literally 'to place a table' used to describe a set up pending a ceremony like marriage, or burial.

îdu̯-ɔ̀kpɔ̀ Literally to give a person a knock with the knuckles.

îfu To see

îfū-nwántà-ézè To be the first to see a baby's first tooth. This is usually celebrated with the discoverer buying a gift for the baby.

îfurènyá Love; 'see eye to eye.'

îfusi-ènyá Suffer.

îgaghà To go past. To cross.

îga To go.

îgbachĭ-nkū To ban the fetching of firewood.

îgbà-ḿpa Be perplexed, confused.

îgbaba-ɔ́mú Literally, 'to tag' with ɔ́mú so as to indicate ownership, and used mostly to indicate

an interest in a young girl to be married.

îgbà-m̀gbá Wrestling

îgba-m̀gbúgbá A ceremony usually after the death of a paramount ruler or prior to an important communal celebration, men of all ages dress in wraps and holding long stakes, dance around the community.

îgba-ŋ́nù̯nù̯ The traditional coming of age and initiation of boys in Ébịrịbá in which the initiate kills a bird, strings it on his bow and walks about naked, except for a belt of twisted copper, throughout the village showing off his game and collecting gifts from friends and relatives. Non-initiates are forbidden from entering the íkòrò house.

îgbà-òg̃ig̃è To give a woman a strip of a man's farmland for her to plant her own yam.

îgbapwo-nkū To lift the ban on the fetching of firewood.

îgba-rị̀-ifẽ To appreciate

(a dancer) by giving money or gift items.

ịgbà-rị̀-ikòrò-ndi To appreciate the Ikoro during ịgwa-máng by giving yam (and drinks) to elders gathered in the Ikoro hut.

ịgbàghàrì Door.

ịgbata To shoot at or sting each other.

ịgbàtà To be neighbours.

ịgbà-ùryè To put a tattoo.

ịgbawa To blow out.

ịgha (1) To turn. (2) To sprinkle. (3) To plant.

ịghɔ̀gbù To deceive. To cheat.

ịg̃ù To count.

ịgwɔ To cure. To heal

ịgwa-máng (1) To appease the gods. (2) Traditional thanksgiving ceremony performed by an Abiriba age grade to mark its retirement from active military/communal service.

ịñàtíñà Equal. Balance.

ịñɔ̀nkí Cantankerous (person).

ịñw̃u To peel (the skin of cooked yam.

ịkà To scratch (with an object)

ịkà-ámá Pre-igwamang ritual.

ịK̃a-ɛ́nyá To be insulting.

ịkàghà A cone-shaped fish trap made of bamboo strips in a wicker form.

ịkɔ̀ To till (the soil).

ịkɔ To scratch (the skin).

ịkɔ́ghɔ́rí A kind of yam.

ịkɔnù (1) To berate. (2) A traditional performance by the Ùkpó community of Ɛ́bịrịbá in which men folks sit at the communal arena to berate anybody that passes by.

ịkɔ̀bàsì Church. Sunday.

ịkɔ̀-ókw̃ù To make earth yam mounds.

ịkɔtɔnù Verbal exchange of words.

ịkpákị̀ A kind of game in which a piece of stick fashioned like a top is spun on the ground and then a whip is used to slap it to maintain a continuous spin.

ịkpánku To fetch fire wood (from the bush).

ịkpákpà Corn.

ịkpàndà Person who stays in the village and would not travel to any place of sojourn.

ịkpàràñwu Not taking a bath.

îkpɔ To buy (pot, sac, bag, cloth).

îkpɔ̀ghɔ́ Flirtation.

îkpɔ̀pwo-éze Chiselling out a gap in the front teeth for cosmetic purposes.

îkpɔta-ɛ́ká An early traditional activity in which girls from one community engage those of another in a bitter repartee which ends in exchange of blows.

îkpɔ-ésè Groan, Whimper

îkpɔ-òkù Invitation to inform of an impending ceremony, etc.

îkpɔ-ɔ́K̃ù Burn; destroy by fire.

îkpu To mold; carve.

îkpụ-ụzũ To go to a place of sojourn for purposes of doing business.

îkpụ-ụzũ Blacksmithing.

îkpù To drink.

îkụ To beat.

îK̃ù-ŋ́dí To give yams to relatives, friends and well-wishers during festivals.

îkùrú-îgwamang Preliminary activities to the traditional appeasement of the gods' ceremony.

îkùrú-ògbò Gift-giving to both the parents and their child named after a person.

îkwa-ɛchichi Sweeping the burnt farmland for planting.

îkw̃atù To demolish. To push down.

îkwɔ To grind

íkwɔ (Of a sharp object) to be worn

îkw̃ɔ-ulwo To plaster the walls of a house.

îkwụ (Of climbing plant) to grow luxuriantly.

îkwụ-ụgwo-ɛ̀kũ To the bride-price.

îlañe-íñw̃ú To continue. Moving forward.

îla-íshí To shave the head.

îñ̃a To dive.

îñ̃aɓà To dive in.

îmù 1. To learn. 2. To light (a fire).

îmù-ɛnyá To keep awake.

înañɛ̃ɓà Traditional age-grade name-taking ceremony.

îna-ŋdi The collection of gift yams and meat by children from their namesake.

înɔ̃-ŋ̃zũzụ̀ To be in training, or in the process of being groomed, (in preparation for marriage).

ĩnɔ̀-ɔ̀mɔ́ghɔ̀ To be nursing a baby.

ĩnwu To die.

ĩnyìnyà Horse.

ĩpa To lift.

ĩpa-apa To be intoxicating.

ĩpaɓà-mádù To inter a dead body.

ĩpamà To consider.

ĩpàrálì Lowly. Low priced.

ĩpĩ-òkìrì To castrate.

ĩpɔ Pottage, with yam, cocoyam or plantain as the main condiment.

ĩrɔ To dream.

ĩrɔ̀ghɔ́m̀béè The act of tricky evasion.

ĩrɔ̀rĩ To be joyous.

ĩrù To plant (àžúmà, beans, etc.)

ĩrù-byóm byóm To walk with the toes due to wound at the heel area.

ĩr̃u To work. To weed.

ĩr̃u-ɛ́fĩfyá Weeding.

ĩryɔ To beg.

ĩsà To answer.

ĩʃa To remove the shuck (of corn).

ĩʃa To wash.

ĩʃu-m̀kpúkpɔ̀ Clearing farmland that had been recently farmed on and usually devoid of trees.

ĩʃu-ɔ́r̃ú Bush-clearing for planting purposes.

ĩʃu-úzɔ- úbì Clearing of the pathway to the farmlands usually a communal effort involving every able-bodied persons.

ĩta To bite.

ĩta-ɛ́tú To chew stick used for teeth clean.

ĩtɔ-ɛ̀kpà (Literally, "opening the bags" to give) gifts to people met on arrival from a travel.

ĩtù (1) To measure. (2) To buy (garri).

ĩtu To carve.

ĩtubà ŋzu ɛ̀'njà Literally, 'putting a piece of white clay chalk in an earthenware pot' signifying that a young woman has been spoken for.

ĩtu-éyè Promulgation of traditional laws to be observed in Ɛ́bĩrĩba in the next year, by the Ɛ̀nàchíòkèn.

ĩtu-ínyìr̃ì To dirty.

ĩtùtù To try.

ĩwá Cassava, (Efik borrowing).

ĩwá-ár̃i Cooked, sliced cassava soaked in water and eaten with coconut or palm kernel nuts.

ĩwá-pànyá A species of cassava with red skin

that could be cooked
and eaten like yam.

ı̈wari-úbì The division of
family farm land
amongst owners
preparatory for its
cultivation.

ı̈wayi-úbì To give out
farm land plots
preparatory for its
cultivation.

ı̂wʉ (1) To buy (crayfish).
(2) To bathe (the body).

ı̂wu-ɦwú To take a bath.

ı̂wʉ-máɗù-ɦwú (1)
Giving a person a bath.
(2) First of the two-day
burial ceremony in
Ébírı́bá.

ı̂zar'ɛ̂ɾà Name-taking
ceremony performed
bv age-grades in
Ébírı́bá.

ı̈zɔ́fɔ̀rɔ̀ Back yard, back
door. Back of the
kitchen. **ı̂nɔ̀-:** to be
menstruating:
(menstruating women
used to stay in the back
of the kitchen.

ı̂zʉzʉ̀-úlwò Painting the
floors and walls of the
traditional mud wall
homes.

j

jà Exclamation equivalent to "good grief" used mostly to express consternation.

jàá Praise, as in: Íjàá íƙé *(to praise)*.

jàá-ŋmama Greeting as used to announce a boy performing ìgba-ŋnùnù.

jáɓàá Goad (somebody) into.

ʝáɓàá Sleep or lie in.

ʝághàá Lie.

jághá-jághá ɔkɔmị̀bà Loud metal clappers used by ɔkɔmị̀bà dancers; Noisy person.

jàrí Pull off (a branch from a tree, plantain, or banana from its bunch).

ʝár̃i Lie.

jàyì Calm. Silent.

ʝèé Go.

jéghéjéghé A feeling of being beat up.

ʝĩ Spit (spittle through the teeth) in a continuous stream.

ʝì Break. Snap.

jí Husband.

ʝì Holds.

jí Be black or dark (of colour).

jí ákw̃u Cassava,- (tuber, or plant).

jìcɦyé Impound, or seize; confisicate.

jíjè Mock. Mimicry.

jìƙér̃ì Get ready; pre prepared.

jìsye-íƙe Strive hard; hang in there; be strong.

jɔ́ Bad.

jɔ́-ɦwụ̀ Lose weight; Emaciate.

jɔ̀njɔ Be bad. Ugly. Evil.

jù Be filled. Full.

jụ̀ (1) Ask (of a question). (2) Refuse.

jù-ɛ́ɦwɔ́ Satisfactory. Be filled, or satisfied (of food).

jù-ɛnyá: Astonish. Surprise.

jùɦú Be cool. Calm.

k

kà Surpass. Greater.

ká Be hard, strong or ripe (of yam, cassava, coconut, etc).

káà Greeting. (Generic term used in virtually all situations involving greeting)

kàá Make a mark.

kàá Be old, or advanced in age.

kàá-ámà The official pronouncement of the laws to be observed in Ébịríbá for the year by the Ènàchíòkèn made at Ámúkú on Íríàmà.

kàá-ékpe (Of a dying man) make last wishes.

kàgbwó Cancel; cross out.

kàñí Get old.

kàñágbà Audacious.

kálá Look at.

kàláryà Coral beads (necklace).

Ƙámà Rather than. But. Instead. Rather (after negative).

Ƙámáɓúɓu A kind of plant with leaves ending in sharp thorns and used as vegetable.

kà-ŋka Grow old. Wear out. Torn.

ká-óbù Without remorse; show courage.

kásyèé Comfort (someone) for a loss.

ká-úkà To scold or rebuke severely.

kè (1) Divide. Share. (2) Break the surface of a hard object eg. break with finger nails usually of both hands, small seed like melon seeds to remove the skin.

ké Shine. -dámdám: shine brightly.

Ƙé Tie; bind. -égbú: bind.

Ƙèchyé Cover with cloth, or paper; Wrap up and tie.

Ƙèé-ìsì Plate (hair).

keé-jí Give a woman in marriage.

keé-ŋdí Harvest yam for the first time by slicing the tuber and leaving the seed-head.

kèé Create, as in: Chíneké *(God the creator)*.

kèékè Deliberate; will to act; on purpose.

kèlé Greet. Salute.

kémkèmkém (Of eyes) darting here and there.

Ƙèŕ̩ị   Arrest; take into custody.

kèwá   (1) Break (with the teeth) (2) divide up, or demarcate.

kéyíí   (Of anger) long drawn out.

kñá-ɛ̀nyà   Be insulting, overbold, or overassertive.

Khálu   (1) The god of thunder. (2) Popular male name in Ɛ́bị̀ŕ̩ibá.

Kñálu   Short for **Kñámálu**, God of thunder. Popular male name.

Kñámálu-ŋde-éɓe   Shrine in the compound of Ńdé-Éɓe, Á̃mógùdù in Ɛ́bị̀ŕ̩ibá.

Kñámálu-ɔ̀z̃ẁà-élu   Shrine in Ɔ̀z̃ẁà, Á̃mámbà in Ɛ́bị̀ŕ̩ibá.

kñáŋkó   (Defunct language person coughing.

kɔ́tùmá   Court messenger. (English borrowing).

kɔ́-ɔnu   Revile. Abuse.

kɔ̀wá   Turning (the sod) preparatory for building.

kú   Have a houseboy, maid, or apprentice.

kù   Blow (of wind from fan or breeze).

Ƙú   (1) Give, as in: Ƙú ŋdí *(give yam)*. (2) Plant (seed). (3) Tap juice,

of Ɔ̀gbụ̀ for) Duck.

Ƙó   (1) Take with a hook. (2) Swell. Dilate. (3) Get in (a fight or extended conflict.

Ƙóƙóshìlóshì   (Standing) away and apart as a show of apathy.

kòròtá   Coal tar. (English borrowing).

Ƙótwòó   Bring down (from a hanging place).

Ƙó-úka   Run afoul (of the law); Get in trouble.

kɔ́   (1) Be scarce (not obtainable. (2) Scratch. (3) Be dry. (4) Till the soil (with a hoe).

kɔ́kɔ́nì   String beans.

kɔ́rɔ́bɔ́m   Tiny measuring bowl.

kɔ̀sɔ́ɔ́   Expression used to commiserate with a

or sap from tree, as in: Ƙú ŋ́gwɔ̀ *(tap palm tree for wine)*.

kụ́   (1) Knock. Blow. Clap, as in: Kụ́-éká *(clap hands or punch)*. (2) Ring, as in: Kụ́-átáng *(ring a bell)*.

kụ́kụ̀bá   Place an arm around (someone's) shoulders.

kúkúŋ̀dà   (1) Stars. (2) Fire flies.

ƘúƘùtá   Scrape the bottom

(of a pot for food to eat).

Ƙ̀ndé Cling on.

kùpwó Knock open; make a hole.

kùrú (1) Hold or carry (a baby). (2) Fetch (water). (3) Take in, as in kùrú-nwánta- ŭ̃ ̀

(*take in an apprentice*).

kúrúmá Crewman (English borrowing).

kùtá Steal (cooked beans or àẑúmá).

kùtwó Knock down.

kùwá Break (anything breakable.

kp

kpà Be associated or friendly (with).

kpá (1) Search for and Gather, as in: Kpá ŋ̌ku *(search for and gather firewood)*. (2) Buy, used in: Kpá mànù *(buy oil)*. (3) Be needful, derived from: Ŋ́kpá *(need)*. (4) Clamp, as in: Kpàchỹé *(clamp shut)*. (5) Apply, (by drawing) a line, as in: Kpá tìró *(apply the eye-pencil substitute)*. (6) Cut. Trim (hair or beard).

kpàá Braid (Hair), Weave (Basket).

kpà-ághá Capture (in a war).

kpàcħáří-ɛ́nya Be cautious. Beware. Be warned.

kpàchỹé Clamp shut.

kpà-ɛ̀k̃ừ Amass, or gather together a lot of wealth.

kpàgbwó Choke, or strangle to death.

kpàkásyá Back-bite; Defamation of character.

kpákwừrứ Clutch (in the hand or under the armpit).

kpálákuku Pidgeon.

kpà-ḿbwɔ̀ (Of rain) drizzle.

kpá-ŋ̃gàŋ̃gà Boast; Behave in a superior, condescending, or arrogant way; Be showy.

kpám-kpám Entirely. Completely. as in: Ɔ́gwula kpám-kpám *(it is completely finished)*.

kpámòtú Tap (on the shoulder) to call attention to.

kpàɗé Clamp; squeeze tight.

kpá-ókè Shift boundary marks, or demarcations (fraudulently); discrimate against.

kpá-òkpòghò Amass, or gather a lot of money; collect money, or wealth.

kpàtá-ɛ́nyà Cheat.

kpát̃ừm-kpát̃ừm A children's game in which players hop along squares marked in a pattern on the ground to pick up a small object thrown into one of the squares.

kpá-ừbỹà Cheat. Take

more than you are due.

kpàyí (1) Speak. Talk.
(2) Strike. as in: Kpàyí
ɔ̀kpá shyám *(strike a
match).*

kpàyírí Tell; spoke to.

kpé (1) Pray. Worship. (2)
Strip off, especially the
skin (of plantain,
banana, orange etc). (3)
Dribble. (4) To act as
Judge.

kpè-íkpe Adjudicate; Try
a case, or give
judgment.

kpèbwòó Make a decision,
final determination, or
judgment of a case.

kpèghéré-kpèghéré
Rough handle, or push
every which way; as in:

kpɔ́- íñw̃u Meet first
thing in the day
(usually tied to either
good, or bad luck.

kpɔ̀-ɔ́ƙu Burn.

kpɔ́-òkù Call, or convene a
meeting

kpɔ̀kátá Call together.

kpɔ́kù Call upon.

kpɔ́m-kpɔ́m A traditional
garment accessory
consisting of two long
strips of screen printed
silk scarves worn
around the neck or
waist.

kpɔ́m-kwèm Exact,

Kw̃á kpèghéré-
kpèghéré *(push
around).*

kpèkpèkpè Motorcycle.

kpékpéré Straight.

kpèryé (Of a man) to have
sexual intercourse with
a woman.

kpĵ Pinch.

kpĵrĵ To steal (especially
small sums, or petty
objects).

kpɔ́ (1) Call by name. (2)
Dry. Be ripe. (3) Take
by inserting in nose, as
in: Kpɔ́ énwỵ̀rỵ̀ *(take
snuff in nose).* (4) Buy,
as in: Kpɔ́ ìtè *(buy a
pot).*

kpɔ́ĝàrĵ Sit, self-
importantly.
perfect.

kpɔ̀nɗé Nail on (to a
cross).

kpɔ́nƙu (1) Cut firewood
(with an axe). (2) Be
dry.

kpɔ̀nw̃úá Wither. Atrophy.

kpɔ̀pwó Pierce. Make a
hole.

kpɔ̀sìí Act like a blind fool;
stupidly.

kpɔ̀ǐé Awaken.

kpɔ̀ǐú Call; Summon.

kpɔ̀wá Split, as in:
Kpɔ̀wá ŋƙu *(split fire-
wood).*

kpụ̀ Mold.

kpụ̀ụ́ (1) Loose interest in (after having had too much of) an item. (2) Eat (garri soaked in cold water).

kpù Wear (a hat).

kpù Pass under by stooping.

kpụ̀kɔ́tá Congeal.

kpùú Capsize.

kpùchṽé Cover up.

kpụ́kpɔ̀ɔ́ Remove completely (roofing material from a house).

kpụ́kpɔ̀ɔ́-ɛ́kà (1) Wipe, or rub the hand together to get rid of anything on them.

kpú kpùtɔ́ Cover; conceal

kpùú kpùú The throbbing (of pain).

kpùpwó Uncover; remove cover; reveal.

kpùrú Wear or cover oneself.

kpùrú- ụ́gbụ̀ Wear a costume as a masquerade.

kpụ̀rụ́ Carry with the mouth. as in: Kpụ̀rụ́ mini ɔ́nu *(hold water in the mouth)*.

kpụ́rụ́kpụ́rụ́ Round and hard.

kpwàá Mould, sculpt, or shape.

kpwàá-ụ́zụ́ Iron, or metal work. Blacksmithery.

kpwòó (1) Pour on (water, etc.). (2) Appear all over or break out (of rashes).

kpwòó-ɛ̀kwụ̀ (In a fight, or wrestling) hold in a neck lock.

kw

kwá (1) Pack, as in:
Kwá ŋgwóŋgwó
(pack belongings).
(2) Cough, as in:
Kwá ụ́kwárà *(cough).*
(3) Buy (items of
clothing), as in: Kwá
ńgwa *(buy clothing).*

kwà Each, as in: Kwà
máɗù kwà égbè
(each person a gun).
Every, as in: Kwà-
ízù *(every day).*

kw̃á (1) Cry. (2) Push.
(3) Tie (wrap or belt)
around the waist. (4)
Mourn, or perform a
wake.

kwàá (1) Slip. as in:
Kwàá étụ́rụ *(be
slippery).* (2) Miss.

kwàá-èchíchí See
èchíchí.

kwàá-ħwù Be
accustomed to.

kwàá-kwàá-chị̀ See,
ákị̀rị̀-ényi

kwàá-ŋgwá Buy
clothing items.

kw̃áɓàá Push in.

kw̃áɗàá Push down.

kw̃á-ħwòó Pour away;
spill.

kwàkpútá (Greedily

chew) in a noisy way.

kw̃á-ɔ́k̃ú (Of gun)
misfire; Failure.

kwápú Pack
(belongings) and
leave.

kwárí Used as a
derivative suffix to
indicate: Back at you,
as in: Mè kwárí
(retaliate), Gwò
kwárí *(take back).*

kwàrí (Of a divorced
woman) pack
(belongings) and
leave

kwàyí (1) Place (in a
basket or big bowl).
(2) Accord (respect).

kwàyí-ŋ̀kìsì Seek
protection from an
assailant; run to
someone for help
from an attacker.

kwèm Straight and
upright.

kw̃ó (1) Be crowded.
(2) Stiff, (used to
describe an erect
penis). (3) Grate
(cassava). (4) Abort
(a pregnancy).

kw̃ònyí Grab hold of.
Seize

kwòó Agree. Accede.

kwòó-ísí Nod head back and forth in agreement.

kwɔ́ (1) Grind (corn or beans). (2) Wash (hands and feet). (3) Carry (a child) on the back.

kwòó-ŋ̀kw̃à Make a promise. Give an undertaking.

kwɔ̀ɔ́ Cut with a saw.

kwɔ̀rṹ-ɛ́kà Wash the hands.

kwɔ̀rṹ-ɛ́wɔ̀ Piggy-back. To ride on the back of another.

kwú (1) Speak (a language). (2) Buy (salt).

kw̃ú Catch (in the act).

kwùá Pay.

kwùá Of climbing plants, hanging in a loop.

kwùá-úgwɔ Pay up on a debt.

kw̃ùá Scrape.

kw̃ùá-èbù Be mouldy, or be mildewed.

kw̃ùgbwó Hang to death.

kwúkwùbá Ball the hand (especially enclosing something).

kw̃ùnyí Meet. Join up with.

kw̃ùpwó Open (a lid).

kwùtáa Kidnap. Steal (mostly domestic animals).

kwùtɔ́ Be stuck, caught, or held in an immovable position; Not able to find a solution, or way out of a situation

kwùwáyí Make a down payment.

l

là (1) Go (home). (2)
Shave completely, as
in: Làá ísí *(shave the
head)*. (3) Raise to
expose. as in: Làá
ɔ̄k̄à̄r̄à *(raise wrapper)*.
(4) Leak, as in: Làá
mini *(leak water)*. (5)
Already, as in: Órì lá
(he ate already). (6)
Bump into (especially
with the shoulders), as
in: Lá ya kpèghéré
kpèghéré *(bump him
around)*.

làá ji Get married.

làá áẓụ Go back, or lag
behind.

làá íbì (Also **làáríbì**)
Go to waste. Squander,
or lavish.

làá-íshì Have a hair cut
(usually a close
shaving).

láɓà Go to bed (to sleep).

làbúkɔ́ Topple over.
newborn; take care of new
baby and the mother.

lèghá Name for
summoning dogs
(usually as an invitation
for the dog to come eat
babies' feces).

lègháryá Look around.

lábùsɔ́ Startle, or scare.

làbúrú Raise up (wrap to
expose).

lághàá Pass by on the way
home.

lághála Imaginary far
place.

làñé Go home.

làkásyá Destroy, or
dismantle.

lá-mini Literally: 'Leak
water'. Develop a fault.

lásàá Disorganize. Put in
disarray.

làwàá Rip. Force to tear,
as in: Làwàá ɔ̄k̄à̄r̄à
*(rip a wrapper by
forcing into it)*.

làyí Contract out.

lèbé Watch.

lèbéchì Look up to God.
(Hope in God).

lèé Look closely.

lèé-ɔ̀mɔ́ghɔ̀ Look after a
woman with a

lèlyá Underestimate.

lèrwó Look closely; pay
attention.

lèsá See.

ñ̥ Thump.

lí Bury.

lìbé (1) Tie, as in: Lìbé
érírí *(tie with a rope)*.

(2) Bury, as in: Lìbé
àlì *(put into the earth).*

lɔ́ɔ́ (1) Throw, as in: Lɔ̀ɔ́
ǹk̃úmà *(throw stones).*
(2) Flog, as in: Lɔ̀ɔ́
ákánchu *(flog with a
whip).* (3) Slimy, (as
used in describing Okra
soup).

l̹kàá Exert enough energy,
or struggle.

lɔ́ɔ́-ɛ́kà Slap.

lɔ́pù Remove (items in or
being roasted in fire).

lɔ́sàá Disorganize
(burning firewood in
the fire place).

lɔ̀wàá Break. Smash, as
in: Lɔ̀wàá ìtè *(smash a
pot).*

lú (1) Slip (of tongue).
Miss (of activity
requiring dexterity). (2)
Buy (drinks).

lú̹ Marry.

lùbé Leave untouched (as
in beard or hair not
shaved.

lúghú̹lu̹ See **ɛ̀kpà-ímí-
ókóghóró.**

lù̹ú̹ (1) Fight. (2) Marry.

lyàá Thump (a person,
usually on the back)
with a clenched fist.

lwàá (1) Fight. (2)
Assume a (wrestling)
position. (3) Come
back. Return home.

lwàá-àlì Assume a down
to earth position.
Reduce oneself.

lwàá-ɔ̀kàlì Assume a
wrestling position
involving going down
on one knee and
scooping the
unsuspecting
opponent's feet from
under him.

lwàá-ji (Of a woman)
Marry, or wed

lwàá-nwámì (Of a man)
Marry, or wed.

lwàá-ù̹wà Return to the
world after death (in a
traditional belief that
dead persons return to
the world in a
newborn).

lwàrị Soft to the touch.

m

má Know.

mà If, as in: Mà ɔ́dighi ŋno *(if not so)*.

màbá Display prominently.

máɗù Person. Somebody. Human being.

màkà Because of. On account of.

màlísá Start.

mámir̃i Urine.

mámi̧r̃i̧-úkú Diabetes.

máng (1) Spirit. Ghost. (2) Fetish often placed in farms or tied around produce trees to deter thieves.

mánú Oil.

mánú-ègbùrù̧ Palm Oil.

mánú-òtíté Cream. Pomade.

mànyí Start

mányí Drinks (generic for alcoholic beverages).

mányí-mini Palm wine.

mányi-ɔ́ƙu Hot (gin) drinks.

mányí-mányí Steamed ground-bean paste usually wrapped in broad leaves. (Yoruba borrowing).

mányí-mányík̀ɔ Water leaf. (Efik borrowing).

mányí-ŋ́ju̧ru̧ First drink presented to a would-be bride's parents by a suitor.

màr̃í Be it known to you; recognize; know.

mází Mister. (Ndizuogu borrowing).

mé Do.

méɓà Put in.

mèbá Make rich.

mèbé Prepare. Make ready.

mèbézyé Repair.

mébì Destroy. Ruin. Spoil. Keep in disorder.

mèchwó Stop.

mèchwó-íñ̃u Humiliate, or disgrace.

mèchỹé Close. Shut.

mèchỹé-ɔ́nu Shut up.

méɗà Put down.

mé-èbérè Be sorry for. Take pity. Have mercy on.

méfàá Make a mess of.

mèǧá Put life into, as in: Mèǧá ħwù *(be lively)*.

mègbú Oppress. Ill-treat.

mègháryá Change. Change position.

mègháryá-ɛ́nyà Deceive.

mèñá Wipe off, as in: Mèñá ímì *(wipe off the nose)*; finish.

mèñé Keep doing.

mèñí Be alive again.

méñwú Spend lavishly.
Waste.

mé-íféře Put to shame.

mèjɔ́ Offend. Wrong. Do
wrong. Injure.

mèjú Fill up.

mèkásyá Spoil. Destroy.
Ruin. Disgrace.

mèkátá (1) Pack up. (2)
Bring disaffection
between two persons.

mèkɔ́ Give to a
satisfaction.

mèkɔ́tá Put together.

mèkwárᵢ̀ Take revenge, or
get even.

mèlyé Raise.

mènɗé Oppress.
Tyrannize over.

mènyí Serve (used
(a person). Defeat.

mèryé Play.

mèrwá Defile.

mèrwá-ñwù̀ Sustain
injury.

mèsí Frighten. Scare.

mètá Quarrel.

mèťé Wake (from sleep).

mètú (1) Touch. (2)
Kindle (a fire).

mèwá Break in two (of
kola nuts).

méyá Do it.

mèzí Do good. Do right.

mézù Complete.

mèzyé Mend; Repair; Fix.

mèzwòó Fulfil.

mí Sink.

especially for soup,
stew and other spoon
based food items).

ményi Blood.

mènyí-égw̃ù Scare;
Frighten; Intimidate.

mènyí-iwo Provoke; cause
to be angry.

ményi-ményi Bloody.
Red.

mènyú Extinguish.

mépàá Make dirty; Soil.

mépù̀ú̀ Pay off

mépù̀ú̀ Get rid of, as in:
mépù̀ú̀-íme (terminate
pregnancy).

mèpwó Open. Declare
open.

mèrí Defeat. Win.

mèryé Win. Overcome

mî̀ (1) Suck. (3) Absorb.

míɓà Submerge.

mí'ghí You and I (Me and
you).

míní Water. Rain. Ocean.
River.

míní-máɗù A person of
calm disposition.

mí-ỹá He and I (Me and
him).

mɔ̀bù Either. Neither.

mɔ́bụ̀ghụ But for. If not
for.

mó'zi Angel.

mù (1) Give birth to.
Beget, as in: Mù nwá
(give birth to a child).
(2) Learn. Teach, as in:

Mù ékwúkwɔ́ *(study)*.

mùɗú Set fire to burn (weed, grass or forest).

múné-múné An almost imperceptible mouth movement.

mùnyí Light (a lamp or fire).

mùsá Be successful (of person studying).

mwóo Myself. Me.

mwàá (1) Learn. (2) Give birth to.

mwàá-ɛ́kwúkwɔ́ Learn from books; study.

mwàá-nwa Give birth to a child.

mɣ̃àá Suck (usually through a straw).

mɣ̃è Wife.

mɣ̃èé Sink.

mɣ̃e-ji (1) Husband's other wife (in a polygamous marriage). (2) The wife of a woman's brother in-law.

mɣ̃e-nwa Daughter-in law. Also used for sister-in law.

'M

'm Me, as in: Ní 'm *(give me)*.

m' I, as in: M' rye yà *(I ate it)*.

m̀ɓá (1) Bitter complaining. Threat. (2) Sizable and whole, as in: Mɓá ŋ́di *(whole yam)*.

m̀bà Faintness. Extreme tiredness.

ḿbà Nation, tribe, or alien land. ónyé-: foreigner. Anybody not from Ɛ́bíríbá.

m̀bádá In the open; in public

ḿbádámbá Width. Flatness.

ḿbà-mini Expression used to describe places of sojourn in riverine areas.

m̀bàrá A kind of edible frog with long legs.

m̀bàkárá White man (Efik borrowing).

ḿbè Tortoise.

m̀bé Mixture made by squeezing a kind of leaf with itchy properties used for fishing. When poured into a river, irritated fish would come to the surface for an easy catch.

m̀bè-m̀bè Shadow.

ḿbè-míní Turtle.

m̀bèrèɡ̃éɗé Suddenness, as in: Ífé m̀bèrèɡ̃éɗé *(accident)*.

m̀bí Dice, token used for playing board games.

ḿbíbí Destruction. Ruin.

ḿbìgbɔ́ Scolding. Storming. Uproar.

m̀bị̀là Water yam *(dioscorea alata)*.

m̀bị̀rị̂ Left; awkward.

m̀bɔ́kɔ̀ A secret society in Ɛ́bịríbá in which a long line of mostly half-clad, old men painted in soot, wearing British police helmet, walk in a single file. The first person holds a big bell aloft, the second person holds a big pot in front of him and the third holds a long pointed spear said to have the magical powers of transfixing a person to a spot if the victim's shadow is stabbed by the spear.

m̀bụ́ First. One, (used in beginning count).

ḿbụ̀ State of rottenness,

as in: *ímà-m̀bù* (To be rotten).

m̀ɓù Drawing of blood with a horn, cup or other shaped calabash from any part of the body to relieve congestion, swelling pain or to get rid of impure blood.

m̀ɓùɓà Brief. as in: Kwá m̀ɓùbà *(brief stay)*.

m̀ɓúɓú Public holiday.

m̀bùbù Rows of tribal marks made on nubile girls as a decoration extending from the neck to the navel.

m̀bùghúnè Calf.

m̀bùm-pùsá-ùwà Birthmark

m̀búzù Cricket.

m̀bwɔ́ Finger or toe nail.

m̀bwɔ́-íkpe Court costs.

m̀bwɔ́-ŋ́kwu The dry skin of a kind of tree used for medicinal purposes.

m̀byàràmbyá Stranger. Squarter.

m̀fághá Tight spot.

m̀fé Easy. Lightness.

m̀fí Periwinkles. One of the several fresh-water mollusks with a black shell. (Efik borrowing).

m̀fífà Angry yell.

m̀fíjoku Shrine set up as the deity responsible

for good harvest, and gets a yearly sacrifice.

m̀fú Vision. The act of seeing (in the future).

m̀gbá Wrestling.

m̀gba A kind of glue, or gum.

m̀gbáɓú A kind of flying ant with a bad sting.

m̀gbàdà A small antelope with short backward-pointing horns.

m̀gbada A kind of xylophone in which wooden stakes placed on a cut banana trunk are beaten to produce sound.

m̀gbàdìghìnì By this time.

m̀gbàdìghìnì-échi By this time tomorrow.

m̀gbàfàtà Narrowed area like the crotch or armpit.

m̀gbàghátá Lies and double-speak. Falsehood.

m̀gbágharì To turn around.

m̀gbáhárì Mercy, or forgiveness.

m̀gbàlà-ŋ́kà See m̀gbàlà-úzù.

m̀gbàlà-úzù Blacksmithing shed.

m̀gbálì Serious attempt, or endeavor.

m̀gbàm (1) Accident

prone. (2) Cooked, ground melon seeds wrapped in leaves (Umuahia borrowing).

m̀gba̱mgbá̱ A kind of fruit with a black skin and succulent flesh.

ḿgba̱nwò Transformation; change; alteration.

m̀gbá̱-òkpúrù Betrayal; conspiracy against.

ḿgbápyá-ŋ́kɔ́lɔ̀ Tonsilitis.

m̀gbàréká Bracelet.

m̀gbà̱rɔgw̃ù Root.

m̀gbàrɔ́kpà Ankle Bracelet.

ḿgbárú A formal condolence visit to a bereaved person.

m̀gbáryà Woven sieve for preparing garri before frying.

ḿgbasi Witchcraft; Sorceress.

ḿgbazi Taking, or giving of a loan; lending, or borrowing.

m̀gbà̱ 1. Time. 2. Threshold. (3) When.

ḿgbá̱ghéré Dilapidated.

m̀gbà̱-ɔ̀ɦ̀ù At the time.

m̀gbà̱-ɔ́rɪ̀ In times past.

ḿgbá̱ré Crooked. Bent.

m̀gbá̱ré Earthen ware pot used for palmwine.

ḿgbá̱mgbá̱ Pawpaw (papaya).

m̀gbà̱ríwò Tadpole.

m̀gbá̱sɪ̀ A kind of stinging black ant.

ḿgbá̱lu Gall bladder.

ḿgba̱ The act of collecting the bark of a certain plant the fibre of which is used for making rope.

m̀gbɔ Bullets; Slugs.

m̀gbɔ́ See **Mgbɔ́tà.**

m̀gbɔ́gbɔ́-m̀gbɔ́gbɔ́ (1) The stalk of an ear of corn. (2) A kind of children game in which smooth stalk is placed between the lips and then slapped out to make a musical sound.

m̀gbà̱ɔŋgbɔ̀ Used in: Ɛ̃́rá-m̀gba̱ɔ́ŋgbá̱ *(breasts of unequal size).* to describe something that is lobsided.

m̀gbɔ́tà Daughter of, as in: Mgbɔ́tà Òk̃ék̃e *(daughter of Òk̃éke).* Female name.

m̀gbà̱dùm A walled off section in a kitchen for housing domestic animals.

m̀gbá̱gho An overstay in a place of sojourn before coming back home.

m̀gbá̱ko Forest, or bush (used only in) ánù̱-mgbóko *(bush animal)* to describe someone stupid

m̀gḅúḍú A kind of snake-
looking multi-coloured
earth-worm.

m̀gbúgbá See ỉgba-
m̀gbúgbá.

m̀gbúpwó Window

ḿkpà Need. Necessity.
Difficulty.

m̀kpà Scissors. Forceps.

m̀kpá Walking stick. Staff.

m̀kpàghà-ɔ́ɓa Wooden
stakes fashioned out of
the Úr̀ù tree used as
gates for yam barns

m̀kpaji Strips of dried
palm fronds used as pin
for making ɔ́g̃ányí.

ḿkpaka Stick; short
heavy club.

ḿkpakɔ Communal farm
land.

m̀kpàǹkpá A kind of
wrestling throw
involving the swinging
of the opponent across
the body.

m̀kpáǹkpá Soup made
with cut up goat
entrails.

m̀kpàrítùm Traditional
dance of the Éḅịríbá-
Ụ̀món society in which
the dancer wearing
high top hat is
costumed with a skirt
of layers of cloth
around the waist and
holding a decorated

staff.

ḿkpátáḿkpá Cut side (of
an animal carcass).

m̀kpe Mourning (usually
for a deseased husband)

m̀kpɛ́'kwụkwɔ Plant leaf.

ḿkpị He (billy) goat.

ḿkpị Half portion. Section
(of seed, nut, etc.)

m̀kpịkpá Ladle.

ḿkpìrìkpì Stump.
Fragment.

m̀kpịsị Any object shaped
like a ramrod, with
pointed tip; Pike; Pen.

ḿkpịsi-ɛ́kà Finger.

ḿkpịsị-ɔ́kpà Toes.

m̀kpòsúm Innoculation
(Efik borrowing).

ḿkpɔ̀ Basket usually
hung by the hearth used
for curing meat and
fish.

m̀kpɔ́ Tree stump.

ḿkpɔ́kɔ́rɔ́ Empty.
Useless.

m̀kpɔ́là Copper rings
formerly used as
money.

m̀kpɔ́rɔ́ Chain.
Imprisonment.
Confinement.

Mkpóró Neighbouring
village close to
Ám̃ógùdù.

ḿkpú (1) Loud cry. Shout.
Cry for help. (2)
Anthill

104

m̄kpúghúrú Headless corpse.

m̄kpùghùrù Piece (of). Less than whole.

m̀kpúkà A small livestock room in the kitchen.

m̀kpṳkpɔ̀ Farmland having been recently farmed on and usually devoid of trees used for planting cassava.

m̀kpṳkpṳ See m̀kpú-mini.

m̄kpṳkpṳ Expression used to describe places of sojourn not close to riverine areas.

m̀kpú-mini Swimming style involving moving under water.

m̄kpúnkpú Expression used to describe places of sojourn in non-riverine areas.

m̄kpúnkpú-àẓù Hunch on back.

m̄kpṳ́ŋkpṳ́ Short.

m̄kpṳ́ŋkpṳ́ Hillock.

m̄kpṳ́ŋkpṳ́-ókw̃ù Yam mound not planted with yam.

m̄kpùpwo Revelation.

m̄kpṳ́rɛnyà Eye ball.

m̄kpṳ́robù Heart.

m̄kpṳ́rṳ Seed. Fruit.

m̀kpúrù Room. Bed-room. Inner room.

m̄kpṳ́rṳ (1) Single piece. (2) A kind of ailment forming small swellings on and around the human neck area.

m̄kpṳ́rṳ-amṳ̀ Ball, or testicles.

m̄kpṳ́rṳma Broad leaves used for wrapping èsṳ̀sù.

m̄kpṳ́rṳ-ósísí Fruits.

m̀má Mother.

m̄ma Beauty. Nice. Good.

m̄mà Knife. -ékw̃u: kitchen knife. -òg̃è: machete.

m̄mà'g̃u See Ìkpìrìkpé-ɔ̀g̃ṳ̀

Mmàkṳ̀ Another name for Ám̃ántà.

m̄mam̄ma Greeting wishing one of goodness.

m̀màr̃ɔ́gw̃ṳ̀ Magic.

m̀mèm̀mé Festival. Fete.

m̄mérí Play. Game.

m̀mùmà Plan.

m̄m̃ĩm̃ĩ Fruit in a pod eaten raw that has a strong smell and a hot taste usually eaten with kolanut.

m̄mùrí The act of sharing small portions (money).

m̄pa Scar; a mark left on skin from healed wound.

m̀pàm Short machete without sharpened

edges used mainly as a prop during traditional war dances.

m̀pàrɛ́ká A small, hand, oil-lamp. Alto hurricane lamp.

m̀pìdì Jumping up and down.

m̀pù Horn.

m̀pù Ability to exercise restraint.

m̀pù-ɛ́kà Elbow.

m̀púm̀pú (Of cheeks) round and fat.

m̀pya Dented or disfigured. (Used in): Ímí m̀pya *(nose partly or wholly disfigured by disease)*.

m̀pyákɔ̀ Corner. Nook. Cranny.

m̃

m̃á (1) Jump, as in: Má ɓà è míni *(jump into the water)*. (2) Beat, as in: Míni m̃á'm *(I was beaten by the rain)*. (3) Wear by tying or wrapping a piece of cloth. as in: Nwók̃e m̃á ɔ̀k̃à̃rà *(the man in a wrapper)*. (4) Used as a derivative prefix: Má íkpe *(sentence or pass judgment on)*. Má égwá *(be homesick; miss)*. (5) Pierce or Stab, as in: Má gbwó *(stab to death)*. (6) Buy, as in: Má éfì *(buy a bull)*.

m̃àbá Tie on somebody (wrapper or piece of cloth).

m̃àbaá (1) Dive into (a river). (2) Dig into (a pocket, or hole)

m̃áfàá Make a mess of by the constant sticking of hands or objects into.

m̃àfé Jump over. By-pass.

m̃á'ghàá Jump across.

m̃àgbwó Stab to death.

m̃á-ìkpìrìkpè Play the drum.

m̃á-ɔ́sw̃à (suck the teeth) to show contempt.

m̃à̃rí Tie onto self (wrapper

m̃ànyí Plant or drive into the ground (a tree or peg).

m̃á-ŋkwà Beat, or play musical instrument.

m̃à̃rí-ɛ́kà Bet, wager, or throw a challenge.

m̃àtá Bump into; Head on collision; Meet.

m̃àtá-ókw̃ù Compete (usually while making yam mounds).

m̃àwá Stab open.

m̃éghém̃éghé Bitter-sweet taste: The kind of after-taste left in the mouth when you drink water following a meal of bitter-leaf soup.

m̃í Bear fruit.

m̃í Dry (over fire, or in the sun).

m̃í-ɛ́g̃u Starve; Deny food.

m̃ìkà Used as a derivative suffix: Ɔ́dì nányìí m̃ìkà *(it was soaking-wet heavy)*.

m̃ím̃àá Pass hand slowly over.

m̃ím̃àgbàtá Pass hand all over.

m̃ìpà Dirtily heavy.

m̃ó Breath.

m̃óðà Exhale.

m̃òr̃ú Inhale.

m̃ú Sharpen, as in: Mú

ŋmà *(sharpen a knife)*.

n

n' Mother of (used as a
possessive marker)
as in: N'Úchè
(Uche's mother).

ná (1) Collect. Take
from, as in: Ná útụ
(collect levy or tax).

ná-e See ŋnà-é

nábàsá Welcome;
Admit; accept.

ná-ɛ̀kà Shake hands.

nàɦá Take away from.

nàɦí Drop or let-drop
(something) by
accident.

námà Cow.

nányí Nine pennies.

nápùụ́ Take away from.

nàɾí Take, or receive.

n'ɛ́ɾɛ̀ Give way.

néji Mother of a
husband. Mother
inlaw. Female
members of a
husband's family.

nénti Imaginary
monster invoked by
mothers to punish
erring children.

ní Give; present.

níɦì Because.

ní m' Give me.

nínì Radiate (of pain).

níŋí-níŋí Sweet (taste).

ǹtụ́ Give some (money,
gift, etc).

nɔ̀ Be, as in: Nɔ̀ úlwò
(be at home).

nɔ̀básá Come (closer) to
someone.

nɔ̀chỹé Usurp. Take the
place of (someone).
Take over.

nɔ̀ghá Stay. Sit.

nɔ̀láɦí Move away.

nɔ̀laɦítụ́bá Move away
some more.

nɔ́mɔghɔ̀ Nursing
mother.

nɔ̀nɗé Stay put.

n'óhèrè Give way.

n'ókóo Imaginary game
play-mate.

nɔ̀pwó Step aside;
Move away.

nu Hear. Understand
(language).

núghụ̀nụ̀ghụ́ Tip.
Topmost.

núnụ̀ Shoot (of a plant).
Tip.

nùɾ̃ú Gather or scoop up.

nùú Push.

nụ̀ụ́ Fire (pottery) in a
kiln.

ŋ̃

ŋá (1) Drive. Ride. Pilot, as in: Ŋá úgbɔ́ *(pilot a ship or paddle a boat)*.

ñàá Tilt.

ŋàá-kpúù-kpúù (Of pain) pulsate.

ñàbúkɔ́ Keel over.

ñàbá ńchì Listen.

ŋáɗú-ŋàɗù-ŋáɗú Exhibit greed (over food).

ŋágbú-ŋàgbù-ŋágbú Confused, stupefying state. Dizzy.

ŋájyé-ɛ́kà Be overwhelming.

ŋànyí (Of traumatized body part) become painful.

ŋányí-ŋányí Expression used to describe frying.

ŋɔ́ŋɔ́-m̀bée A kind of long-beaked bird that crows mostly at dusk.

ŋèé Cross or go over (a gutter or raised object).

ŋèé-ɔ̀kparíshí Swing leg across, or over (someone's) head.

ñéghàá Cross over.

ñîñàá Tilt around

ŋ̃íŋàs̩íñá (Of utensils) rinse.

ŋ̀ùàá-mang Take an oath; swear.

ñùrî Merriment; pleasure.

ŋ̀ùŕú (1) Borrow. Hire. (2) Drink up.

ñùrvá Merriment

ŋ̀ùtú Take a drink; have a sip (of water or other beverage).

ŋ̀ùú Drink.

ŋ

ńchà Soap.

ŋchà óru Home made black soap said to have anti-rash medicinal qualities.

ŋcħaȓa Rust. Colour of rust. Rust coloured silt deposit used as paint in mud wall decorations.

ŋché The act of keeping awake, especially in order to protect or guard.

ǹché-ánwú Umbrella.

ǹché-ísí Pillow.

ńcħì Ear.

ŋchì Grass-cutter - a burrowing rodent.

ŋchìchí Flat wooden bat used as trowel and for flattening wet earth during building.

ŋcħì-έɓù Purulent, ear infection.

ŋchí-ὲkwà Woman - no longer a teenager.

ŋchìghá Shelving forming the ceiling in traditional kitchens serving as storage area.

Ŋcħìná One of the age-grades in Έbìȓíbá.

ŋcħì-íƙe Hard of hearing. Deafness.

ŋcħìȓì-áƙi Broken shells of palm kernel nuts.

ŋcħì-ŋƙìta A kind of dark to reddish brown crunchy mushroom that looks like the ear of a dog.

ǹcħúcħú Earthen ware pot used for storing palm oil.

ŋchụmáng A kind of herbal spice.

ńdándá Small ants noted for dragging loads out of proportion to its size.

ǹdáà How?

ŋdé Those of; Those who; People of, as in: Ŋdé Áᵯántà (Amanta people).

ǹdéwòó Common salutation.

ńdí Yam. Food.

ŋdí-éwù Stalk and leaves of a particular shrub used as goat fodder.

ŋdí-ìƒe People; Human beings.

ŋdí-míni-ɔ́ƙu Yam pepper-soup.

ŋdɔ́ (Expression meaning): Serves you right.

ŋdɔŋ Jigger. Chigoe flea which penetrates the skin of mammals and makes her home beneath the surface to feed and produce eggs.

ńdù Life. Alive.

ŋ̀dúdù Feeling of general malaise following abuse of the body due to excess work.

ŋ̀dúgbòm See **nwá ŋ̀dúgbòm.**

ŋ̀dùghú 'Your Life': (Used when someone sneezes to indicate): 'Bless You'.

Ŋ̀dùm Another name for Ámógùdù.

ǹdùmɔ̀dù Advice. Instruct.

ǹdùm-ńtà Dragonfly

ǹdùrú Pigeon.

ǹdùrú Shade.

ŋ̀dwɔ̀mdwɔ́ A general free-for-all scramble for something.

ŋ̀g̃àng̃à Showy. Fashionable.

ǹgàrì Bribe.

ńge One.

ǹgèlé Small stream.

ŋ̀ghìghé Batch or set, as in: Ŋ̀ghìghé ŋ́ge *(one batch of)* fried garri.

ǹgînị What?

ŋ̀gịnị̃ *Slang word:* Used in answer to an Ɔ̀'gíni - question deemed by the addressed as not worth answering.

ŋ̀gòlòbí Strong smelling, meat, or fish product used as seasoning. (see ɔ̀lɔ́gbù-óko)

ǹgɔ̀lɔ̀pí Weak and lazy.

ŋ̀gɔ́zí A blessing. Mostly a female name.

ŋ̀gú A long stick with a hooked end for harvesting, or plucking fruits.

ŋ̀gù̀ Curdled oil preparation used for eating certain foods like three-leaved yam, plantain, shredded cassava etc. It is prepared by crushing some quantity of potash *(àkáwá]* in a small amount of water and pouring it into palm oil in which some condiments like fresh pepper, crayfish, salt etc. are added. The preparation is then stirred until a required curdled consistency is achieved and it is used as stew.

ŋ̀gú-ɛ́kwù̀ (1) Pointed stake used for removing palm nuts from the bunch. (2) Protruding (teeth).

ǹg̃ùg̃úr̃u-úde Cobwebs.

ŋ̀gùzó Temporary stopping.

ŋ̀gwá (1) Quick. Haste.

Swiftness. (2)
Clothing. Attire.

ǹgw̃áà This way.

ŋ́gwá-áfya Merchandise,
Goods.

ŋ́gwágha Ornamental
metal, or copper
footwear for maidens.

ŋ́gwá-ágha Weapons of
war. Armament.

ŋ́gw̃ághá Ornamental
ringlets worn on ankles
and wrists mostly for
brides from rich
families.

ŋ́gw̃á-ŋ̀gw̃à Quickly.

ŋ́gwóŋgwó Things. All
sorts of things.

ŋ̀gwɔ́kɔ̀ A kind of yam
characterised by a
deformed, twisted tuber
that sometimes sticks
out of the ground.

ŋgwɔ́kɔ̀ŋgwɔ́ Used as
adjective to describe:
Intertwining, twisted
movement.

ŋ́gwɔri Yam meal
prepared by mashing
cooked yam together in
plenty of palm oil with
various ingredients.

ŋ̀gwú̧ To be Completely
finished. Used in, íri-
ŋ̀gwú̧ (*to eat to the last
piece*).

ŋ̀gwù̧gw̃ɔ́ Act of scooping
unnecessarily large
portions of a sauce in a
meal.

ŋ́gw̃ùgw̃ù Parcel. Bundle.

ǹgwú̧'ŗ̌ų Lame or Cripple.

ŋ̀gw̃ù̧ŗ̌ù̧ Lizard: (General
term for mostly *agama-
agama*).

ŋ̧̀jà A small earthen ware
pot.

ŋ̧̀jà-ígwò Wide iron pot
used mostly for making
garri.

ŋ̧̀jàkìrì The exchange of
playful, or joking
remarks between
people in a
conversation.

ŋ̧̀jàŋ́jà A kind of
vegetable leaf with
medicinal qualities.

ŋ̧̀jé A kind of disease
affecting babies
characterized by
diffuse lesion and
inflammation of the
anal opening.

ǹièm Journey, travel, trip.

ŋ̧̀jèm -ɔ́kɔ́chì Journey
performed by Ébị́ŗíbá
people in which they
travel home from their
various places of
sojourn around the end
of every year.

ǹìí Blackness. Darkness.

ŋ̧̀jìghí̧ŋ̧jì Inflammation of
the joints. Arthritis.

ŋ́jikeŗ̌e State of readiness;

Preparation.

ńῖílá Snail.

ŋ̀jʲílá-ὲgbà A species of snail - brightly coloured and not usually edible.

ŋ̀jó Badness. Wickedness. Ugliness.

ŋ̀kà Art. Craft, as in: Ónyé ŋ̀kà *(artist, craftman, painter or sculptor).*

ńka Old age. Oldness.

ǹk'á This. This one.

ńkághárị̂ Rag: tattered

ŋ̀kághárị̂-ŋkagharị Raggedly.

ŋ̀kàkásị̂ To bad-mouth. Criticize. Assasinate the character of.

ŋ̀kákwu Long snouted musk rat.

ŋ̀k̃ám Tail (usually of an elephant) as in ŋ̀k̃ám-ényi elephant tail.

ŋ̀kàkásị̂ Defamation, of slander.

ŋ̀káráfɔ́ng Rust (Efik borrowing).

ǹkàsị̂ Cocoyam.

ǹkàtà A kind of round basket.

ǹkè Belonging to.

ŋ̀kélu A kind of small bird; kingfisher.

ŋ̀k̃eři Taking a person away; arrest.

ńkèwá Division.

ŋ̀kìkére Shell, as in:

Ŋ̀kìkére ŋ̀jʲílá *(snail shell).*

ǹkị̂rị̂ Hot tempered.

ńkị̂sị̂ Silk.

ŋ̀kìsì The act of seeking protection from an assailant; run to someone for help from an attacker.

ńkị̂ta Dog.

ŋ̀k̃ò Any gadget with a hooked end for bringing down out-of-reach items.

ŋ̀kóróbá Brassiere. (Efik borrowing).

ŋ̀kɔ́ (1) Sharpness. Intelligence. Nimbleness. Acuteness. (2) By the side; corner; angle.

ŋ̀kɔ̀ Belch. Burp, as in: Íbù ǹkɔ̀ *(to belch).*

ŋ̀kɔ̀gbé (Of knee) knocked, bent or crooked).

ǹkɔ́kɔ Crab.

ǹkɔ́lɔ̀ Throat.

ǹkɔ́lɔ̀-ɛ́kpù Goitre.

ŋ̀kɔ́lɔ̀-ryóghóryóghó To tantalize.

ŋ̀kɔ́m Spoon (Efik borrowing).

ǹkɔ́m-éze Fork

ŋ̀kɔ́m̀gb̤è Porch, or Verandah

ŋ̀kɔ́nkɔ By way of the side.

ŋkɔrɔ   A kind of nocturnal, burrowing, edible insect.

ŋkóróbá   Brassieres (Efik borrowing).

ǹkù   Wings.

ńƙú   Wood. Firewood.

ŋ̀ƙùkò   Trouble. Troublesome.

ŋkúkú-òkèn   Ball shaped rubber container with a syringe for an injection of liquid into the rectum.

ŋkùƙúr̃ùbè   Shoulders; part of the arms by the neck.

ǹƙúmà   Stone. Rock.

ŋkṵ́tṵ́   A hammer with a wooden head.

ŋkṵju   To hail. General greeting to a group.

ŋkṵ́wá   A deep cut (made in a wood so that when hit on the ground would split the wood).

ńkw̃à   Promise.

ŋkwà   Musical instruments.

ǹkw̃á   See ŋkw̃á-lèbé.

ŋkw̃á-lèbé   Piece of stick used as a projectile.

ŋkw̃ànyí   A kind of sweet-tasting yam.

ŋkw̃á-òbù   Elaborately carved Ékpè hut statues

Ŋ̀kwɔ́   A market day following Àfɔ̀.

ǹkwɔ́   Saw.

ǹkwɔ́   Kite.

ŋkwɔ́cħá   Bereft. Bald, as in: Ísí ŋkwɔ́cħá *(bald-headed)*.

ŋ̀kwɔ́-èƙùmà   Shrine of two, large copper-bound stones in Ám̃éƙe on which warriors who had killed in a war front are received and made to describe their prowess and are then cleansed before demobilization.

ŋkwɔ́fỹá   Bruising of the inner thigh caused by walking friction.

ńkwú   Palm tree.

ŋkwùkwó   Water yam porridge cooked mostly in ceremonies involving the cleansing of a child who had falled into a communal toilet.

ŋ̀là   Bug found mostly in dried fish.

ŋ̃lebùtá   Rivalry. Competition.

ǹlú   Repeat, or recur.

ŋ̃lùghà-ŋ̃lùghà   Disorderly. Unkempt.

ŋ̀lùlù   Tendrils and general shrubbery growing across forest pathways and tending to entangle the legs of passersby.

ńnà Father.

ńnaɓàsá Admission.

ŋnàbɔ̀ Traditional dance (Efik borrowing).

ŋnà-é 'My Father!': Exclamation of surprise, pain, wonder, etc.

ŋnà-ji Father-inlaw. Any male member of a husband's family.

ŋnàńnà Grandfather. Male name.

ŋnaǹńam-ògbú-m̀pàm Praying mantis.

ŋnà-úkú Boss. Husband. Master.

ǹné Mother.

ǹnékwú First wife.

ǹnéǹné Grandmother.

ŋnéǹném-ìtè-óšò One of the traditional masquerades of the Ùkpó people of Ébíríbá.

ŋné-ɔ̀mɔ́ghɔ̀ Nursing mother.

ǹní Like this.

ǹníná Troublesome.

ǹnó So.

ńnɔ Toilet.

ǹnú Salt.

ŋnụ̀ Four hundred; large number.

ŋnú-ènwò A kind of sweet fruit that leaves a lingering sugary taste in the mouth.

ńnụ̀nù Bird, (generic).

ńnúnu Apex; Tip.

ńnúnu-ɛ́r̃a Nipple.

ŋnụ̀nụ̀-èrè-ɔ́dù A kind of bird with a multi-coloured tail.

ŋnù-núghị̀rị̂-nu Uncountable number.

ǹǹùrù Borrowing.

ńrɔ́ Dream.

ńrìsá To remember.

ŋrụ̀rụ́-àlì Metal pipes stuffed with gun-powder and set-off like a canon.

ǹshá Comb.

ńshí Poison.

ŋ̃shí Faeces. Dung. Excreta.

ŋsíbírí Script of the cult language of Ekpe society and its masquerades.

ǹshí-ègbè Gun-powder.

ŋshí-nwámì Venereal disease.

ŋsị̂sà Shredded cooked cassava that has been soaked in water used for making trditional salad.

ŋsɔ́ (1) Holy. Sacred. Abomination. Avoidance. (2) A woman's period of menstruation.

ŋ̃sòghòr̃àžú Follower. Successor. Back person.

ńs̃ù Loss.

ŋ̀sụ̀ Stammering. Stuttering.

ŋ̀swó Nearness. Proximity of. Close.

ǹswɔ́-èbùlù Somersault.

ŋ̀tá A kind of children's disease characterised by excessive weiht loss and a depression along the middle of the head.

ŋ́tá Hunting; organized hunting expedition.

ńtà Small.

ŋ́tá-ŋ́kpụ̀rụ̀ A kind of hunting in which a portion of a bush or forest is cordonned off and animals in the area chased with loud noise and sound towards an opening where they can be trapped.

ŋ́táchú A kind of mushroom.

ǹtáƙi Eel.

ŋ́táng-ŋ̀kàǹdà Ostrich feather used in hats for decorative purposes.

ŋ́tàntá Any form, or kind of edible or chewable meat treat.

ńtárú Antidote.

ǹtèntè A kind of insect.

ŋ̀tìkóró A small gourd container used as a safe.

ńtìkpìrì Half. Piece.

ŋ́tíńtí Short and fat.

ŋ̀tó The telling, or revealing (of something secret. The act of snitching, or ratting on.

ŋ̀tófo Fishing net, (Efik borrowing).

ńtụ́ Ash.

ŋ̀tụ́ A yellowish inscrustation on the teeth, chiefly calcium phosphate.

ŋ̀tụ́ Number, or frequency of times.

ńtúbe Hole. Empty space.

ŋ́tụ̀m A kind of fruit with tangy salty taste.

ŋ̀tụ́mànụ̀ Stewed stockfish.

ńtúǹtụ̀ Ashy, or dusty.

ŋ́tụrì The act of sharing tiny pieces of (meat or fish).

ŋ́tụr̀íí Aimless walking (about); loitering.

ŋ̀tụ̀rụ̀pá Pulley type small animal trap.

ŋ̀tụ́tụ̀ The act of picking up the last pieces of crumbs.

ńtụ́tụ Many. Much.

ŋ́wéyí An item of clothing; Cloth; dress; garment.

ŋ́wúté (Of an experience) being painful).

ńza Since.

ńz̃a A kind of small bird

ŋ̀zè-ébùlù The bearch of a ram used for traditional

dances.

ŋ̄z̄íz̄í Borrowing, as in: Ịgba ŋ́z̄íz̄í *(to borrow).*

ŋ́zu White chalk of deposited silt given to visitors as a sign of welcome.

ńzùkɔ́ Meeting. Council.

ŋ́zùkɔ́tá A gathering together.

ŋ̀zúzù Stupidity. Idiocy.

ŋ̄z̄ùz̄ù Training. Grooming, as in: Nwágbɔghɔ̀ nɔ́ ŋ̀z̄ùzù *(girl being groomed for marriage).*

ǹzùzwó Hiding.

ŋ̀zwòmzwó Game of hide and seek.

nw

nwá   Child.

nwàá   Clear the throat to cough up (phlegm).

nwáɗa   Young woman; Miss.

nwá-èbè   Carved wooden figurine.

nwáfifì   Squeaking dolls or statues used by traditional medicine men.

nwá'm   Mv child.

nwágbɔghɔ   Girl. Maiden.

nwàĥí   (Of cloth) become faded; common place.

nwáji   Half brother or sister. Paternal cousins.

nwáji-èzí   Persons of the same compound or hamlet.

nwámì   Woman. Female.

nwám̀bá   Pussy cat.

nwámgbèyì   (1) Orphan or destitute child. (2) Homely person.

nwá-ŋché-úlwò   Wall-gecko.

nwá-ŋdúgbòm   'Lucky you' (used to refer to a person that finds things easy).

nwántà   Small child.

nwántà-úlwò-ɛ́kwụ́kwɔ́   School child.

nwántà-ụ́žụ̀   Apprentice.

Boy. Maid.

nwánne   Brother or sister (of the same mother but not necessarily of the same father). Term of address for a close friend or person of the same tribe or country in a foreign land.

nwánžụ̀žụ̀   A young person (usually a woman) who receives help, guidance, training, and support from somebody who is older and has more experience or influence.

nwɛ́kà   Girl slave eventually married into the family.

nwò   (1) Own, as in: Nwò òkpòghò *(have money)*. (2) Husk (the seeds of an ear of a corn). (3) Put up, as in: Nwò ɔ́g̃ánví *(thatch a roof)*.

nwɔ́ĥwúřu   New baby.

nwɔ́là   Ring.

nwóřè   Male. Man.

nwókoro   Man. Boy. Youth.

nwụ   Die.

nwú   Shine. Bright. Glare.

nwúghà   Die and leave behind. Bequeath.

nwúnwàsyá-ɛ́nyà   Glare at.
  Open the eyes very
  wide.

nwʊ̀r̃ʊ́   Catch. Grip. Grab
  (a small animal or
  chicken etc.).

nwùr̃ú   Light up.

ny

nyàá (1) Stick, as in:
Nyá ḿgba *(gum up)*.

nyàá Pull, as in: Nyà
jyé *(pull to snap)*.

nyàá Baske, as in: Nyàá
ɔ́ƙu *(warm oneself)*

nyàá Suffer from, as in:
Nyàá ὲkwṹkwṹ
(suffer from epilepsy)

nyàá Wear (necklace,
chain, or any item)
around the neck

nyàá ὲlwà Be seriously
ill.

nyàá-ísi Be arrogant;
stubborn.

nyábwòó Break (items
like bread, or bar of
soap) in two (usually
with both thumbs).

nyàchṹé Patch, plug up,
or close with a filler.

nyàjyé Break.

nyájìpú Break off.

nyàndé Glue onto; stick
on.

nyáƙúnyáƙú Sticky to
the touch.

nyàŕí Hang (around the

neck or shoulder).

nyàndé Adhere to.

nyìgbú Be overloaded.
Heavy laden. Load to
death.

nyìí Climb.

nyị̃ To be beyond (a
person's) power.

nyị̃gbị̃jí Be heavy, or
weighty.

nyìí Be heavy or
burdensome.

nyìƙúŕú Climb onto.

nyịnyị̃ŕị̃ŕị̃ Plentiful (of
people).

nyịsị̃bá-ὲnyà Shut eyes;
close the eyes.

nyòó Peep. Spy. Look
through (telescope,
microscope etc).

nyùú (1) Squirt. (2)
Ooze.

nyùú Set (dislocated
bone by massaging).
(4) Massage. (5)
Pass (wind or feces).

nyùñú Extinguish. Go
out. Die out (of fire).

nyúŕú--gbɔ́rú Cholera.

O

ó' Suffix used at the last word of a sentence as an emphasizer.

ò' A morpheme used in turning a verb into a noun, as in: gbú *(kill)* to ò'gbú *(killer)*.

ò At. In, as in: Ó'bù *(at heart* or *in mind)*.

òbé Cross; post.

óbígwò Metal rod used to dig up yam.

óɓíná Maiden dance of the Ámántà people.

óbìrì See **Íbìri-óbìrì.**

òɓò A large gourd or calabash.

òɓòghímì Nose bleed.

òɓòm Aggressive zeal.

òbú Meeting shed or hut.

óbù Heart. Chest.

òbù A kind of large bird known to soil its underside with its own feces.

òbúbú (1) Dwelling. (2) Carrying.

òbùbù Termination. End.

òbúbú-ághá Cenotaph at Úgú-éʑì in Ébíríbá.

óbù-èbwɔ́ɔ Doubt; indecision (being of two minds).

òbú-ezi Compound meeting place.

óbù-íƙe Confidence.

óbù-íkpútú Stubborn.

óbùláa Ended (of fighting).

óbù-ŋƙúmà Hard-heartedness.

óbù-ɔ́jɔ́ɔ Malice. Wickedness.

óbù-ɔ́ƙu Hot-tempered.

óbù-ɔ́má Kind. Goodness.

óbù-tímtím Pounding heart (due to fear or excitement).

óbù-úcħa Pure hearted.

óbù-ùtwó Happiness; delight.

óbwókɔ́ƙu Fiery coal ash.

òbwòsí Tree producing a kind of bud the base of which is round and used by children to make eyeglasses.

óbyògw̃ú Rough shrub with long prickly stems.

óché Chair. Stool. Seat. Bench.

óché-éɓù Bubo in the armpit.

óché-ézè Throne.

óché-úkà Low wooden stool used mostly in the kitchen.

òchíché Waiting. Guarding.

òcħícħí Blockage; termination.

òchírĩ Small food bowl made of clay used mostly for serving soup.

óchú Farmland that has just been burnt in preparation for tilling.

óchỹè Old. Ancient. Aged.

òdò Yellow; color of gold.

òdódò Yellowish.

òdwó Pathway (usually made by cutting through a forest).

òdúm Lion. **òfèké** No-good. Fake.

ófĩ Pumpkin fruits and leaves.

ófó Sauce. Soup prepared with vegetables, meat and seasoning. Stew.

ófó-ékwúkwó Soup made of leafy vegetables.

ófófó Land cultivated after other farmers had harvested and left the arca.

ógbè Palm fruit bunch without the fruit.

ògbèlé Stream on the road to Ameke farm land.

ógbèyì Poverty. Poor person.

ògbó Name sake. Person having the same name.

ògbòdò A destructive masquerade of the Ámógùdù people.

ógbón Boxing; exchange of blows with knuckles.

ògbón Can. Tin. Metal container.

ógbóro Piece of wood or stick used to tether domestic animals so that they can drag it around without going too far off or getting lost.

ógbóro-ónu Lips.

ógbósígbó Threshold.

ògbú Depth. Deep. Capacious.

ògbú-agù Leopard or tiger killer. Male name.

ògbú-éfĩ Ox killer. Name given to a person who has performed the traditional ceremony of killing an ox for a dead parent.

ògbú-mádù Murderer.

ògbúù Killer.

ògè Long matchet. A heavy knive.

ógè Time. Time span. Opportunity.

ògélè A hollow metal instrument giving a deep resonant tone when struck; gong.

ògèré (1) Afternoon. (2) (Send a child for) baby-sitting.

ògèré-òwù High noon.

óghe See **óghere.**

óghere Opening.

òghòròmà Discomfort.

ògì Semi liquid cereal made with corn flour.

ógìdì Raised pathway or roadway.

ògìrí Fermented oil bean, castor, or melon seeds, used as spice.

ògírisí A kind of sacred tree *(new bouldia)* much used as a live fence and mostly used as a symbolic marker for sacred spots.

ògòri Word (usually not in polite use) for a housewife.

óg̃o Village. Town. Country.

óg̃o-úbì Farm settlement.

ógù A piece of wood used for oath making to prove one's innocence, as in: Éjìm ógù *(I am innocent)*.

ògùrù Yellowish brown inferior palm oil left over from washed out palmnut fibre.

ògùgù Gully; Pit; Trench.

ògúgu A kind of edible, earth-burrowing insect.

ógùmágàlà Chameleon.

ògúmògú A kind of musical instrument made out of a gourd or wooden box in which short pieces of flexible metal are attached on the edge of an opening and plucking them produces guitar sounds. Xylophone.

ógwò Trunk of a tree usually placed at a community arena used for seating, or in the bush latrine for squatting.

óg̃wóg̃wó Massive.

ógwò-ŋ́nɔ Long tree trunk held up by forked sticks low enough for people to squat on it to defecate.

ógwò-sìmén Long cement seat at a community arena - the modern day ógwò

óg̃wu Thorn. Sharp bone.

óg̃wumà A kind of children's ailment.

òhébèghè Slang name for home made hot (gin) drink.

óñwú Twenty.

óñwù Slave.

óñwú-là-ìrí Twenty and ten (Thirty).

òjébárí 'Everybody' (Used to hail everybody among members of a secret society – a mispronunciation of the Efik *oje bap*).

óji Bed. Earthen-bed.

Ójighiri-ŋɗù One of the age-grades in Ébíríbá.

ójíi Black. Dark.

òjíŋgwa Someone who is excessively interested in fine clothes and elegant appearance.

òjò Deserted emptiness (of a house, compound or village).

ójó-ɔ́nu Brim or edge.

òjúkwu A highly esteemed variety of palm producing bright red fruits and said to be efficacious when used as a medicinal antidote.

óƙé Male.

óƙé Big. Great, as in: Óƙé maɗù *(great or big man)*.

ókè Boundary. Mark or Line of demarcation.

òké Rat.

òkè Portion. Share. Division. Allotment.

òkè-àl̞ì Boundary; border; Entire portion of a family land.

òkè-bèkèé Rabbit.

òkè-éfi Bull;

óƙe-ikpo Male lizard.

òƙèn Enema.

óƙé-ɔ̀chi̞chɔ́ Greed.

óƙé-òkpòrò Bachelor; Unmarried man

óƙé-òshì Dysmenorhea.

óƙé-ósísí Another name for the Ɔ́jì tree.

óƙé-òvi High fever.

òké-ɔ́fva Bush rat.

óƙé-ɔ́fya Jungle, or thick forest.

óƙé-ɔ̀kúkù Cock

óƙé-ɔ̀nu Costly. Expensive. High price.

óƙé-óz̧u (1) Corpse of a rich or titled man. (2) Rich person.

Ókèzyé One of the age-grades in Ébíríbá.

òk̞ìkè Creation, as in: Chúkú-òk̞ìkè *(God the creator)*.

òkìrì Castrate (Used in) I̞pi̞-òkìrì *(to castrate)*.

óko A kind of tree sometimes regarded as sacred whose tender leaves are used in food preparation.

óƙò An Ear of, as in: Óƙò i̞kpákpà *(an ear of corn)*.

òkó See òkótà.

òkòbòdí Long animal skin drum. (Efik borrowing)

òkó-émaŋ Traditional masquerade of the Ègbɔ́ji people.

ókóghóró Hole.

ókóghóró-ímì Nostrils.

óƙómóƙó Pompous.

òkòmíso An all-women dance, usually for women of substance.

124

òkóŋgw̃ṳ̀ (Slang for) old man.

òkó-òkó Flower.

òkòp-únènìké Traditional dance of the Ókèzyé age-grade.

òkóró Boy. Youth. Young man. Male name.

ókoro The state of remaining unmarried (usually applied to a divorced woman).

Òkóróntà One of the subdivisions of Ám̃ék̃e in Ébị́rị́bá.

òkóró-òkoro Wild cocovam.

òkóró-ɔ̀byà Youth. Adolescent boy. Young man.

ók̃òr̃ù Likely to start trouble or bring about a mishap.

Òkóryè Male child born on an órvè day.

òkóryè-ɔ́cñá Flower.

òkòsó A playing top fashioned out of a snail shell or metal made by a blacksmith.

òkótà Son of.

òkóyoghoyò (of children) the act of showering under water from a roof gutter during rain.

ókpèrè-ɟ̀wa Cassava stem.

ókpètè Tall perennial true grasses, including sugar cane.

ókpì See ókpìká-ŋkpá

ókpìká-ŋkpá A stout stick or staff. A short thick club.

ókpìrìkpè A rough length of tree trunk or fire log.

òkpòghò Money. Wealth. Manilla (which served as a form of money among certain West African peoples.)

ókpòghóró Shell (of a tortoise, coconut, etc.).

ókpókóró Table (Efik borrowing).

ókpólu Palate.

ókpómà Shark - a kind of fish with strong teeth.

ókpómpí Glutton.

ókpórìmá Shackles; Chains.

ókpóró Walk on foot.

ókpóró-íñw̃u Brow.

ókpóró-ụ́zɔ̀ Main road.

ókpòròkò Stockfish (Efik borrowing).

ókpù Stoutness. Bigness, as in: Ísí ókpù *(big head)*.

òkpú Hat. Cap. Cover.

ókpu A kind of fish.

òkpú-áğu A kind of woven wool hat that tapers to a ball worn mostly on traditional ceremonies and popularized by the traditional war dancers.

òkpú-ézè Crown.

òkpùkpù Multiple. as in: Òkpùkpù èbwɔɔ *(times two).*

òkpùkpú (1) A subterranean cave or grotto. (2) Under the surface opening or activity (of a sore that seems to have healed on the surface but still festering under the skin).

òkpúrù Under. Beneath. Bottom. Underpart.

ókpúrúkpú (1) Dried red mud usually from the walls of a collapsed building. (2) Fallen family house.

ókpúrúmáz̃ù Hump of the back.

òkù Invitation. Feast. Call.

òkù A variety of yellow Guinea yam.

ókwú Word. Language.

ókw̃ú Cover. Lid.

ókw̃ù Yam mound.

ókw̃úcħí Cork. Stopper. Lid.

òkwúkwó Agreement. Assent.

òkwùrù (1)Afterbirth, or foetal membrane, which includes the placenta; (2) The

viscera (of an animal).

òkwùrù-ǹné-ɔmɔghɔ Ailment peculiar to nursing mothers and known to be fatal after a bout of what seems like an epileptic fit.

òlé Which?

òlé-ɛ̀fɲfyá Sanitary inspector.

òlígbù Bitter.

òlílé-ɛnyá Hope and anticipation.

òlìlì Burial.

òlìlì-óz̃ú Cemetery.

òló Hide and seek.

ólú Neck.

ólu One.

ólú-ŋ́kpa Long neck usually with ridges.

òlúlwó Swallowing. Devouring.

òlúù *Ikoro* talking drum player.

òméndi Name given to a large producer of yam. Male name.

òménkà Artist. Male name.

òméȓálì Custom. Tradition.

ómétá Quarrel.

òmétáƙi Unripe palm fruit nut, usually white and as succulent as a coconut.

òmìmì Deep.

ómó Shoot of a plant,

usually just as it is sprouting.

òmúmé A yearly traditional village feast in Ɛ́bị́rị́bá concerning the whole community but with individual villages alloted days in which to cook and invite friends and family from the other villages. Melon seed food items feature prominently, including as soup thickeners, and some cooked in the form of dumplings.

òmùmé Action. Act. Conduct.

òmùmé Ache.

ónúbúrú A kind of rainbow coloured lizard.

ónwo Abscess; boil; pus-filled.

ónwò There exists; He (she; it) has

ònwò Does he (she; it) have?

ònwó Self.

ònwóm Myself

ònwóghu Yourself

ópòtó-ŋ̀kàsì Cocoyam leaves.

òpòtóró Broad or wide (leaf).

òpù Horn. Flute. Pipe. Any wind instrument.

òpyó Dagger.

ònwóghù He (she; it) does not have.

ónwòн̄ù He (she; it) has.

ónwóni Some, as in: Ónyé ónwóni (*some person*).

ónyé Person. Somebody. Person of, as in: Ónyé ós̃i (*thief*).

ònyé Who is it?

ónyé-áfya Merchant. Trader. Customer.

ónyé-ɛ́bỹanyì Visitor

ónyé-ɛ́ká-ébe Witness. Surety.

ónyé-ɛ́ra Mad person.

ónyé-ìchỹè Adult. Elderly person.

ónyé-н̄н̄н̄é Crazy person.

ónyé-ísí Leader. Boss.

ónyé-mbà Stranger. Foreigner.

ònyòghònyóghó-ótò-ákw̃ụ Giant mosquito with unusually long legs found mostly at the base of the iroko tree.

òpété Space. Chance.

ópópó A large wedge-shaped machete.

ópóró Shrimps (Efik borrowing).

óн̄óн̄óн̄ó-ŋ̄ĸu Smoldering wood serving as faggot.

óróntó A kind of smooth-skinned lizard.

óròrì A small cave dug under mud beds in kitchens where

domestic fowls sleep.

órú Far distance.
Imaginary distant place.

Óryè Market day
following ÈK̃é.

óryè-ákw̃a Square in the
center of Abiriba that
used to be a motor park.

òsérélú A kind of fish that
constantly stays close
to the surface of the
water.

ós̃hí Theft.

óshíshí Tree. Stick.

ós̃ò Pepper.

óso Tse-tse fly.

ós̃ó-ɛ́K̃á The long rib
section of a butchered
animal.

ós̃ó-ŋ́kpʉ́nkpʉ́ The short
rib section of a
butchered animal.

ós̃ò-ŋsi Alligator pepper.

òsì Message usually from
the rulership (for the
generality of the people)
delivered from
compound to
compound, as in: Ịsà
òsì *(to broadcast a
message)*.

ótè-írí Dancer.

Ótè-írí Traditional
masquerade of the
Ám̃ógùdù community
of Ébịrịbá with feathers
on the head, sac
costume, and holding

cow tails which are
constantly thrown at
women who end up
paying fines of yam for
being so marked.

òtéríkáng Lantern (Efik
borrowing).

ótii Word used to call
attention before starting
an oral story usually
followed by Ɔ́yɔ̀ said
by members of the
audience.

òtòkòlòghò-ŋ́gw̃ùgw̃ù
Large parcel.

ótópogho See úgbɔ̀ghɔ̀-
èmúmà

òtù Group.

ótùbè Navel.

ótùlà Buttocks. Anus.

ótùtù Callus - the
hardened thickened
place on the skin.

òwù Cry of lamentation
usually aimed at one
who had committed an
abomination.

óyi (1) Cold. Chill. (2)
Dirty. Ugly in
appearance.

òyèrè Resembles, as in
òyèrè-ŋ́nàyá
(Resembles the father);
Female name.

òyé-ɔ́K̃ú-ɔ́fyá Literally,
*One who lights up the
forests*; slang name for
a hunter.

128

òyóyò Beautiful. Fancy.

ózéghịzé (Of a ceremony)
Lively and full of
people.

ózí Message. Errand.

ózú Corpse. Carcass.

òzùgbà All

Ɔ

ɔ́ (He) (she) (It) is.

ɔ̀ (Question marker) Is (he) (she) (it)?

ɔ́ In, At, as in: Ɔ́'ɓa (*at the barn*).

ɔ́ Third person personal pronoun; he; it; she.

ɔ́bà Calabash; Bowl made of gourd cut in two.

ɔ́ɓa Yam barn.

ɔ̀bàbáà Yeah (men), as in: Ŋdé ị̃sù ɔ̀bàbáà (*yes members*).

ɔ́bà-ɛ́ħwɔ Abdominal tumor.

ɔ̀bàsị̀ A god (Efik Borrowing).

ɔ̀bàsị̀-ékpè Statue or tree in front of an Ékpe hut which a masquerade salutes before dancing.

ɔ̀bịlà Ugly.

ɔ̀bɔ̀n Traditional secret society open only to males and usually played at night.

ɔ́bù Pit; Pit trap; Ditch.

ɔ́bụ (1) But. (2) It is.

ɔ̀ɓụ́ɓà To grab.

ɔ̀ɓụ́ɓụ A kind of caterpillar with hairs that sting and irritate the skin.

ɔ̀bùbwɔ̀ Dissection (of animal).

ɔ̀bùbwɔ̀ (Of day) breaking, or dawning. Chí-ɔ̀bùbwɔ̀ (*the breaking of the day*).

ɔ̀bùbwɔ́-àlì A small animal known to make marks on the ground which it retraces to its abode.

ɔ̀bụ́bwɔ́-ị̂wa Cassava farm.

ɔ̀bụ́ụ̀ Crayfish (Efik borrowing).

ɔ́bwɔ̀-ɛ́kà Palm of the hand.

ɔ́bwɔ̀ghɔ́bwɔ̀ Dark orange coloring derived from a wild tuber used for body coloring.

ɔ́bwɔ̀-ɔ́kpà Sole of the foot.

ɔ́bwɔ́-ŋ́mà Scabbard. Sheath.

ɔ́cha Swamp.

ɔ́cħá White. Pure. Undefiled.

ɔ̀cħí White caterpillar found in Kola nuts, eggplants. etc.

ɔ́chị̀ Laughter. Mockery.

ɔ̀chị̀-ághá See ɔ̀chị̀-ɔ̀g̃ù

ɔ̀chị̀cha Cockroach.

ɔ̀chị̀chá A kind of crunchy golden coloured fruit in a

fuzzy brown pod.

ɔchị̀chî̀ Governance.

ɔchị̀-ɔ̀g̃ù War leader. General.

ɔchɔ́'g̃ù A person looking for a fight.

ɔ́chị̀ù Murder. Manslaughter. gbwòó:- Commit manslaughter.

ɔ̀chị́úchị́ú-ɛ̀jà Shrine.

ɔ̀chị́ù Pursuer.

ɔ̀chị́-gádàgádà Name of a masquerade noted for pursuing onlookers all over the place.

ɔ́dàchị̀ Stumbling block; Obstacle; something that blocks a person's path.

ɔ́dị̀ Be (available). Is.

ɔ̀dị̀dà Fall, or collapse; failure; setting (of the sun).

ɔ̀dị̀dɔ́ Earthen-ware water-drinking pot.

ɔ́dì-égw̃u Be tragic. Be wonderful.

ɔ̀dị̀-ŋma Well being. Prosperity.

ɔ́dì-ŋma It is (nice) (fine) (good) (beautiful).

ɔ́dụ Pestle, Pounder.

ɔ́dụ́ Ivory bracelets made from an elephant tusk.

ɔ́dụ Advice. Exhortation. Warning.

ɔ́dụ Tail, as in: ɔ́dụ námà *(cow tail)*.

ɔ́dụ Stall. Shed. Place of business.

ɔ́dụ̀dụ̀ Tail.

ɔ́dụ̀m Lion

ɔ́dụ̀-ŋ́kpíríkpɔ́ A kind of hollow-stemmed cluster tree with narrow leaves used mostly for indicating boundaries.

ɔ́dúwá Boiled corn meal wrapped in leaves.

ɔ̀dwɔ́ Another.

ɔ́fà Antidote.

ɔ̀fɔ́ Justice god usually represented by a small wooden stick of the same name.

ɔ́fyá Bush. Unihabited country. Jungle. Forest.

ɔ́g̃ányí Roofing thatch (made of raffia palm fronds.)

ɔ̀gàzù Guinea fowl.

ɔ́gbà Stone paved area in barns where yam tubers are laid out for drying before being tied to the stakes.

ɔ̀gbáà Shooter.

ɔ̀gbá-ɛ̀jà Diviner; soothsayer.

ɔ̀gbá-ɛ́Ƙú Slang name for women, alluding to their having pubic hair.

ɔ̀gbá-ɛ́kwụ́kwɔ́ Writer; scribe; secretary.

ɔ́gbá-kpụ́rụ̀rụ̀ Appendicitis.

Ɔgbá-ŋje From Gbá ŋje:
*(make several trips-
visits to and from a
place)*. Literally:
Maker of several trips.
Child believed to
belong to a band in the
world of spirits to
which he or she returns
in infancy from there
he goes back to the
mother's womb to be
born again only to die
and go back to the
world of spirits in
infant.

Ɔgb'ɛ̀sì Evening.

Ɔgbɔ́ Arena; Centre of a
circle (of people).

ɔ́gbʉ́ Fig.

ɔ́gbú Leash.

Ɔ̀gbʉ̀ One of the
communities of
Ámɔ́gùdù in Ɛ́bíríbá
comprising of Agbo
Ɔ̀gbù and Ɛlu Ɔ̀gbʉ̀.

ɔ̀ghɔ́m Accident; mishap.

ɔ̀gĩ̀rĩ̀gà-ɛ́nyà Brazen.
Bold.

ɔ́gɔ̀ Inlaw.

ɔ̀gɔ̀ndúm Sewing
machine shuttle.

ɔ̀g̃ʉ̀ Fight. Fighting. War.

ɔ́g̃ʉ Sum. Number.

ɔ́g̃ʉ̀ Hoe.

ɔ̀g̃ʉ́rʉ̀ A kind of rat.

ɔ̀g̃ʉ́ʉ̀ (1) Counter. (2)
Singer. (3) Reader.

ɔ́g̃ʉ̀-úkú Hoe with a giant
blade used mostly by
migrant farm workers
from Ìbĩ̀.

ɔ̀gwà Swamp.

ɔ́gw̃ù Medicine. Charm.
Juju.

ɔ́gw̃ù-áК̃i Seed with
purgative properties.

ɔ́gw̃ù-ɛ́kw̃u Camphor.
Moth balls.

ɔ̀ñà Everybody. Public.
Masses.

ɔ̀ñ̀ù That (one).

ɔ̀ñ̀ʉ̀ñ̀ɔ̀ The act, or process
of making a selection,
or choosing.

ɔ́ñ̀ʉ̀wá An all-women
dance.

ɔ́ñw̃u Cliff.

ɔ́ñw̃úr̃u New. Newness.

ɔ̀ià Flute. Pipe.

ɔ́jĩ Kola-nut. Anything
presented in the place
of kola-nut.

ɔ́ĩ̀ Iroko tree.

ɔ́jì-áwúsá Kola nut
species with no more
than two cotyledons.
Also called ɔ́jì gwɔ́rɔ̀.

ɔ́jì-ìgbò Kola nut species
with more than two
cotyledons.

ɔ́ĩ̀ gwɔ́rɔ̀ See ɔ́jì-áwúsá

ɔ́jì-ùg̃ò Kola nut with
white cotyledons.

ɔ́iɔ́nkwʉ̀ See Át́ú.

ɔ́jɔ́ɔ Bad. Evil.

ɔ́iú If he(she) refuses.

ɔ́kà Fence.

ɔ̀kà Mightier. Greater.

ɔ̀kà-élu Ace climber.

ɔ̀kákáà Almighty.

ɔ̀ká-ŋ̀tṵ̀ Unusually smart (used to describe someone who keeps trying to outsmart others).

ɔ̀K̃àr̃à Wrapper cloth.

ɔ́kàyì Jungle. Forest.

ɔ̀káʒu Vegetable leaves from a climbing plant usually cut into tiny strips and used mostly in traditional salads and special soup.

ɔ̀kḭ Slang name for home made gin.

ɔ̀kḭka Another name for òkó-émaŋ, the traditional masquerade of the Ègbɔ́ji people.

ɔ́kɔ́ Itch. Rashes.

ɔ́kɔ́chḭ Dry season.

ɔ̀kɔ̀chḭ Derogatory term for a woman who is not a member of any group. A non-achieving woman.

ɔ́kɔ́chḭ End of year; period when sojourners go home to Ébḭ́rḭ́bá village.

ɔ́kɔ́chḭ-úkú Fourth year in Ébḭ́rḭ́bá at which time the three major ceremonies of Ízarer̃a,

Ígwamang, and Úche are performed. This has been reduced to a biennial event.

ɔ̀kɔ̀mḭ̀bà Traditional dance group characterized by the use of two large animal-skin drums. This is a mispronunciation of the Efik Ekɔmɔ-Iba

ɔ̀kɔ́nkɔ̀ Masquerade.

ɔ̀kɔ́ŋkɔ̀-átáng Traditional masquerade of the Ékpè society characterized by wearing a knit multicoloured costume and a bell around the waist.

ɔ̀kɔ́nt'èlèmèlé Move round rapidly. Spin around.

ɔ̀kɔ́tɔ́ (In wrestling) the humiliating victory sign placed on the forehead of a thrown opponent.

ɔ̀kɔ́yḭ Comedy. Comic. Funny.

ɔ́kpà Leg.

ɔ́kpà-ébì Filariasis. Elephantiasis.

ɔ́kpà-ŋ́gbéré Knocked-knee.

ɔ́kpà-ŋ́tàŋtṵpárḭ̀ (Of a person) easy to bully,

or pick on.

ɔ̃kpà-ŋ̀ʈíńʈì A kind of mushroom with long stalks said to taste like chicken.

ɔ̀kpàrá Prostitute (Efik borrowing).

ɔ̀kpàrîjè Fast paced walking.

ɔ̀kpá-sᵛám Matches.

ɔ̀kpɔ́ Tiger fish.

ɔ̀kpɔ́ A knock on the head with the knuckles.

ɔ̀kpɔ́ghɔ́rɔ́ Key. Padlock.

ɔ̀kpɔ̀kɔ́ Pipe for smoking.

ɔ̀kpɔ̀kɔ́rɔ́ Empty

ɔ̀kpɔ́kɔ́rɔ́-ékpém Empty bottle.

ɔ̀kpɔ́kɔ́rɔ́-ɛ̀kpà Empty sack.

ɔ̀kpɔ́'kpɔ́ Wood-burrowing insect found in rotted wood

Ɔ̀kpɔ̀kpɔ̀ɔ̀ Traditional dance of the Ámântà community of Ébìrìbá in which a small heavily decorated cloth hut with two children, one holding a life white cock, on top is carried around. The dance was borrowed from the Efik people of Cross River State and brought to Ámântà by Chief Onuma Kalu Emeaba of Ìŋdé Òkórígwò,

Ámântà.

ɔ̀kpɔ̀ndú A kind of game in which palm fronds tied like a broom is thrown and a player tries to catch and pull it down from mid air with a kind of lasso.

ɔ̀kpɔ́nwúr̃ú Tough.

ɔ̀kpɔ̀ɔ̀ (1) Rubber. (2) Bicycle (Efik borrowing)

ɔ̀kpù Bottom; Buttocks; Base.

ɔ̀kpù Morsel (of foofoo).

ɔ̀kpú-íshí Barber.

ɔ̀kpùkpɔ́ Fire place made in the men's house.

ɔ̀kpúkpú Bone.

ɔ̀kpúnyàng Medicinal herb used mostly by nursing mothers.

ɔ̀kpùrùkpù Large piece.

ɔ̀kpùrùkpù Palm fruit with an unusually large kernel nut and little flesh.

ɔ̀kpúù Potter.

ɔ̀kpù-ứtàr̃à Morsel of foofoo.

ɔ̀kpù-ùz̃ù Blacksmith; iron-monger

ɔ̀k̃ú Fire. Hot.

ɔ̀k̃ù Hobby. Profession. One's stock-in-trade.

ɔ̀k̃ú-ébi A ruined condition of yam, cassava, etc., caused

mostly by overheated
soil.

ɔ́k̃ú-àl̃i-ŋ́mɔng Hell
(Ɔ̀h̃áfyá borrowing).

ɔ́k̃ú-íh̃w̃u Carbide-
powered lamp attached
attached to hats and
used for hunting.

ɔ́k̃ú-mang Disease
(especially of children)
accompanied by spots
on the skin.

ɔ́k̃ú-ɔ́kpà Feet burn
caused by sun-heated
sand.

ɔ́kwá Post. Position (of
authority).

ɔ́kwá Wooden platter,
bowl, tray for cutting
up meat.

ɔ̀kwà Partridge.

ɔ́kwá-ŋ́ʐu Wooden bowl
containing white chalk
used for welcoming
guests to a home.

ɔ́kwá-óʂò Wooden bowl,
usually containing
pepper sauce and used
for presenting kola-nuts.

ɔ́kw̃ár̃á (1) First son. (2)
Principal. Main.

ɔ́kw̃ár̃á-ŋ̀kɔ́kɔ Crab or
lobster claw.

ɔ́kwú̧ Stopper (of a bottle
or gourd).

ɔ̀kwù̧ Traditional
masquerade of the
Ám̃ántà people.

ɔ́kwùrù̧ Okra.

ɔ́là Jewelry. Female name.

Ɔ́lara Drinking spring
water behind Ŋ̀dé
Ɔ̀lùghù in Ám̃àntà.

Ɔ́lara-Ám̃ék̃e Name of a
long stream in Ám̃ék̃e.

ɔ́lárá-mini Small gully
made by flowing water.
Gutter.

ɔ̀lɔ̀ghɔ̀rɔ̀-ɛ́k̃á Another
name for Ɔ́lárá-
Ám̃ék̃e.

ɔ̀lɔ́gbù-óko Rancid fish
product used as spice
for cooking mostly
vegetables sauce.

ɔ̀lú̧lú̧ The act of getting
married.

ɔ́má Good, fine, nice,
pretty, beautiful.

ɔ́mà Embrace or hug, as in
Íbỹè ɔ́mà *(to embrace
or hug).*

ɔ́màr̃íme The inner
succulent part of fruits
etc., minus the skin.

ɔ́mìk̃o Compassion. Pity.

ɔ̀mɔ́ghɔ̀ Period
immediately after a
woman's safe delivery
till the baby stops
breast feeding.

ɔ́mú Young palm fronds.

ɔ̀mùmú (1) Stretch marks.

ɔ̀mùmú Child birth.

ɔ̀m̃úm̃ú Heap of (pounded
yam, cassava, etc.)

ɔm̃ùm̃ú Whetting stone.

ɔmừrừnwá Interest on borrowed money.

Ɔnárúbì One of the age-grades in Ébịṛịbá.

ɔnɔ̀dị̣ Seat. Seating. Condition. State.

ɔ́nu Mouth.

ɔ́nu Price of

ɔ̀ɲị̀ɲà Overzealous interest and show of love for (a person).

ɔ́ñù Joy. Rejoicing.

ɔ́nú-áfya Price. Market price. Cost.

ɔ́nú-ɛ́sụ Beach. Seaport. Wharf.

ɔ́nú–ikiк̃e Expensive.

ɔ́numà Male name; the mouth knows

ɔ̀nừmà Severe displeasure. Sorrowful.

ɔ̀nừmà Severe

ɔ́nụ́máṛikwu A single village group linked by a common maternal ancestors

ɔ̀nùnù Heart-burn.

ɔ̀ŋụ́ŋụ́ Drinking. Drink. Drinking party.

ɔ́nụ́-ɔg̃ụg̃ụ Number. Total. Sum.

ɔ́nú-ɔ́jɔ́ɔ Rudeness.

ɔ́nụ-ɔma (1) Polite. (2) Cheap price.

ɔ́nụ́-ụ́gwɔ̀ Front end of a boat.

ɔ́nụ́gwo Short piece of woven cloth in either white or blue, worn by traditional war dancers.

Ɔ́nwá Moon. Month, as in: Ɔ́nwá ésà *(seven months or seventh month).*

Ɔ́nwá-ŋ̀jḛ̃-ghị̣ni Literally "month of no where to go" (usually the rainy season months of the year) when there is no outside activity like farm work.

Ɔ́nwà This.

Ɔ́nwanì This one.

Ɔ́nwú Death.

Ɔ́nwúchi Death according to one's destiny.

Ɔ́nwú-ékechì Natural death.

Ɔ́nwú-íк̃e Unnatural (accidental) death.

ɔ̀nwừnwà Temptation. Trial.

Ɔ́nvá Sore.

Ɔ́nyà Trap. Snare.

Ɔ́nyà ígwò (also ɔ́nyà éze) Gin trap; a mechanical trap designed to carch an animal by the leg using spring operated jaws with a serrated edge.

Ɔ́nyìbá One of the age-grades in Ébịṛịbá.

ɔ̀nyụ́nyụ́ Diarrhea.

ɔ̀nyụ́nyụ́-ŋ̃ší Anus

ɔnyúpà Cheap.

ɔpyà A kind of machete originally used in war, but now used for bush clearing.

ɔ́rĭ That.

ɔ́rĭ-áni That one.

ɔ̀rĭrá-ɛ́ɓúɓừ Edible palmnut chaff removed after palm oil production.

ɔ̀rĭrĭ Thinking. Thoughfulness.

ɔ́rɔ̀ Staleness (as of food left overnight).

ɔ̀rɔ̀ghɔ́ŋma Kwashiorkor; one of the more severe forms of protein malnutrition caused by inadequate protein intake.

ɔ́rɔ́tɔ́ghɔ́-ụ́kà Witty, sarcastic or clever in speech.

ɔ́r̃ụ́ Work. Task.

ɔ́rụ́ Fault. Weakness (of behaviour in human beings).

ɔ́rwá Clay; mud; marsh.

ɔ̀s̃á Squirrel.

ɔ̀s̃ár̃á The external layer of the fronds of the Ŋ́gwɔ̀ tree used mostly for tying yam in the communal barns.

ɔ́shà A kind of musical instrument made in the form of a small basket with a broken gourd base containing small stones for sound.

ɔ́shà-ŋ́tà A kind of bird known for its tightly-woven nest.

ɔ̀s̃ĭ Hissing sound made through the teeth used mostly to call somebody's attention or shoo domestic animals away.

ɔ̀s̃ìsà Answer.

ɔ̀s̃ĭsá Wide. Broad..

ɔ́sɔ́ The act of running; Race.

ɔ́sɔ́-ŋ́dừ Flight for one's life; Refuge.

ɔ́sụ́ A kind of edible breadlike formation used as a filling for ground melon seeds to be moulded for cooking.

ɔ̀sụ́kwụ A variety of palm fruit with light green and fruity nuts usually succulent and producing more oil. Succulent. Juicy.

ɔ̀sụ́-wòwò Used to describe the Ogbele river, it literally means 'cascade.' A stone water fall built, or formed so that water descends over a steep rocky surface.

ɔ́s̃w̃à Sucking the teeth, or

making a hissing sound to show disgust

ɔ́tá Shield.

ɔ̀tàbìrì A kind of rope trap for small animals.

ɔ̀tàgbùlàghì-nɔ́mɔghɔ̀ Centipede.

ɔ̀tá-kwóm A kind of ant that tends to have its head yanked off when it bites.

ɔ̀tá-mmàkwừ Mishap. (Used in) gbáɓa ɔ̀tá-mmakwu ɛkárɔnu *Run into mishap*.

ɔ̀tá-ŋgbímgbí Expression used to describe the act of ignoring somebody talking to you.

ɔ̀tánjélé Bright blue glittering hard stone retailed in small bits used as cosmetics. The stone is crushed on a clean surface, ground into fine powder kept in a bell-shaped aluminum container with a narrow neck and a stick dipped inside the container and allowed to show at the top over the brim. The woman shakes the container to properly stain the stick, then apply the narrow strip of the dark blue powder

to each of the lower eyelids.

ɔ̀ṭighị̀tɔ́ghɔ̀ Any insect/critter, real or imaginary as used to care children trying to be bad.

ɔ̀ṭịsị̀ The symbol of unity and right to rule.

ɔ̀ṭịsị̀-Abiriba The source of authority of its holder as a ruler.

ɔ̀ṭịsị̀-Binyom A form of god of the Binyom people used mostly for extracting the truth from guilty parties in a dispute.

ɔ́tɔ́ Uprightness. Straight. Vertical.

ɔ̀tɔ́ Nakedness. Nudity. Bareness.

ɔ̀tɔ̀ Pottage made by cooking grated water yam with condiments.

ɔ́tú-ényì Small circles of friends formed within an age-grade usually after *igwamang*.

ɔ́tụ̀la It is enough, as in: Ɔ́tụla ŋnù *(there is enough salt)*.

ɔ̀tụ́r̃ụ́ A kind of tree, its wood.

ɔ̀tụ̀rụ̀kpɔ́ High jump.

ɔ̀tụ̀rụ̀kpɔ́kpɔ́ Woodpecker.

ɔ́tụ́tụ́ Many. Plenty.

Several.

ɔtwɔ́-níŋí-níŋí Sweet-
tasting. (Any soft
drink).

ɔ́wá A piece of cut
Bamboo.

ɔ́wá-ŋ̀mừ Torch tinder
made of a special tree
stem, beaten to a fibre
and used to light a fire.
Also used for snail-
hunting.

ɔ́wá–ŋ́nɔ The soft inside
of a palm tree frond cut
in 10-inch lengths used
to wipe the anus after
defecation.

ɔwừwá (Of glasses and
other breakables) The
act of breaking.

ɔwừwá-ányánwu Rising
sun; East.

ɔwừwá-íshí Head ache.

ɔ́yɔ̀ Answer said by the
audience following a
story-teller's beginning
statement of Ótii.

ɔ́yɔ̀ghừyɔ̀ The bunch, or
cluster of particular
fruits

ɔ̀zà (1) Horse or cow tail
hair used by dancers.
(2) Hair on the ear of a
corn.

ɔ́za Thrift association in
which members
contribute money
which is shared at the
end of the year or
season.

ɔ̀zàrà Farmland, usually
not suitable for farming.

ɔ́zɔ̀ Gorrila.

p

pàá (1) Carry. (2)
  Intoxicate.
páɓà (1) Carry into. (2)
  Inter.
pàbúrú Raise up.
páɗà Carry (something)
  down.
pághà Carry across.
pàgháryá Carry around.
pàlá Carry home.
pàlyé Lift up.
pàmàá Give a thought.
  Consider.
pánɗé Help hold on to (by
  carrying).
pánꞋ Bucket (English
  borrowing).
pànyá (1) ÉbꞋrꞋbá name
  for the Spanish
  speaking island of
  Equitorial Guinea
  where some sojourners
  never came back. (2)
  The act of executing an
  enemy of the
  community - thus
  sending the person to a
  place of sojourn where
  return is impossible.
pànúù Carry away.
pàr'ɔ̀bà A draw; usually
  in a competition,
  tournament, or game,
  when the participants

reach a stalemate—
where one did not have
an upper hand over the
other.
pé Trim (the fronds of a
  palm tree).
pꞋ Squeeze. Knead.
p̃Ꞌ Carve. Shape wood
  with a sharp instrument.
píɓà Squeeze into.
pꞋbúrú Cease to squeeze.
pꞋchỹé Close by pressing
  down hard.
pꞋfàá Make a mess of by
  squeezing and sticking
  fingers in.
pìgbwó Strangle.
pìgháryá Squeeze around.
  Knead.
pìkà Soft and messy.
píkàá Feel around (by
  touching).
pìnɗé Squeeze on.
pípꞋ Squeeze out. Drain
  (an abscess).
pìwá Break apart by
  squeezing.
pó Exfoliate (the skin) as
  in scalding or bruising.
pòghò-pòghò Buxom.
pòghórópò Big for
  nothing.
pòó Chamber pot.
pópóru A tree producing a

kind of pod which children fashion out to use as flute.

pɔ́ŋ Unit of currency—pound sterling.

pɔ̀tɔ̀ Soft, messy and sticky.

pɔ̀tɔ́pɔ́tɔ́ Wet, muddy soil.

pɔ̀tɔ́pɔ̀tɔ̀ Soft and mushy.

pú (1) Germinate. Sprout. (2) Spring a leak. Have holes. Be perforated.

pù Get or go out. Escape or pass inadvertently (of fart or faeces).

pùbé-ɛ́kà Form the hand into a fist.

pù-èpú Has a leak.

púghú-pùghù-púghú Shabby (of clothing or parcel). Not done right.

púpùsá (1) Germinate. (2) Burst forth.

pùsá Come out; appear; emerge.

pwó Germinate.

pwó-éze Cut teeth.

pyá Squash.

pyàtá-pyàtá Farm Land not cultivated and overtaken by events.

pyé Movement (in a bush).

r

rá (1) Pass the tongue over the suface of. (2) Plaster (a wall).

ŕá Make love to, or have sex with (a woman).

ràá Suck on, or eat fruit

ŕàá Lead on (usually with intent to deceive).

ràá-ényà Close and reopen the eyes quickly (used to show contempt, or rebuke).

ràá-ĥwú Be difficult.

ràgbwó Lick it all.

ŕàĥí (1) Sleep. (2) Thicken (soup).

ŕàĥúŕà Go to sleep.

ràĥwó Lick and leave some over.

ŕáĥwùú Lead astray.

ràrí Lick off.

rásàá Have (an edible item) licked without order.

ŕásàá Have (a woman) sexed without order. burnt.

rèsá Sell and bring the proceeds.

résàá Sell without a particular order.

rèyí Sell to.

rì Ate.

rì (Be) drowned.

Gang rape.

ŕásiĥá (1) Eat the last of (usually by wiping the bowl, or plate with the last morsel); (2) Completely lick up.

ŕàtá Have sexual intercourse with each other.

ràtú Taste (with the tongue).

ré (1) Sell. (2) Rot. (3) Dance display.

rèbé Tolerate.

ŕèé Be burnt.

rèé (Of medicine) be efficacious and potent.

règbwó Sell all.

ŕègbwó Burn to death.

réĥwùú Sell for less than it is worth.

rèká Dance around (in joy).

rèkásvá Sell at a loss.

ŕèkásyá Completely

rị (1) Crawl (as of snakes, ants, etc.). (2) Think.

ríɓà Crawl in.

rìgbwó Eat all.

rìĥwɔ́ Eat and leave some.

rìkásyá Eat to waste.

ríkègbàtá Blunder about.

ríkèé Blunder.

rị̀kúrụ́ (1) Crawl up. (2) Think over. Make up (one's) mind.

rị̀pù Crawl off.

rị̀pụ̀sá Crawl out.

rị̀rị̀rị̀ Unusually sweet.

rìtú Eat a bit.

rị̀sá Remember.

rìsá Win (a trophy).

rísàá Eat without order.

rìzɔ́ɔ́ Forget.

r̃ó Be in enmity.

ròkóròkó Jelly-like.

rɔ́ɔ́ Dream.

rɔ̀pɔ́yị̀ Say something smart. or witty.

rɔ́ɔ́-ńrɔ́ Dream dreams

rɔ̀tɔ̀ Dirty.

rụ́ Plant (áẓúmà, beans, etc.)

r̃ú (1) Work. (2) Weed (a farm).

rú (1) Reach. (2) Make soft (of palm fruit and pear) by burying in hot ash.

rùbé Threaten to rain (of dark clouds hanging overhead).

rùbé-ísí Be loyal.

r̃ùgbwó Do all (work).

r̃ụ̀ñwɔ́ Work and leave some over.

rùká-rùká Lukewarm (water).

r̃ùkásyá Do a bad job. Destroy.

r̃ù̀sá Earn. Word and be rewarded.

rùtá Argue.

r̃ụ̀tụ́ Try out work.

rwàá (1) Plant (beans, okra). (2) Be ineffective (of talisman or iuju).

r̃wàá Work.

rwàá- àlì Commit an abomination, or sin against the earth.

rwòó Make soft (as in roasting African pear in hot ash.

rwòó Reach, or arrive (at a destination).

ryé Eat.

ryé-mini (Of goods) Destroyed by water.

ryé-ŋchà (Of cloth) Worn threadbare.

ryɔ́ Beg, as in: *ryɔ́-árìryɔ́* (beg, especially for forgiveness; a plead for mercy.

S

š́á Wash. Scrub.

sá (1) Open (hand, book).
(2) Pass. Come (by
the way of), as in: Sá
ŋ̀gw̃á *(pass by this
way)*.

sàá Give answer; Reply;
Retort.

sáà Exclamation of
displeasure. Shut up.
Be quiet.

sàá-ɛ́kà Open the hand.

sá-ŋ́za Ever since

š̀àká Tear.

sàpó Sponge. (Yoruba
borrowing).

sàɳwó Open (the eyes).

š̀àr̃í Tear off.

sáṣ̌ĩ́ḿá Wash completely.

sá-ŧà As from today.

sàyí Announce, as in:
Sàyí-òsì *(make an
announcement)*.

sósù Exclamation to shoo
away (any of domestic
animals e.g. goat, fowl
etc.)

sé Draw. Pull. Stretch.

séɓà Pull in.

séɗà Pull down.

sérélu Float.

sèrí Pull. Draw towards
self.

sépù̀sá (1) Pull out (of

person) from (a room).
(2) Be lured into
trouble.

ṣî Say. Tell.

ṣìnĩ̀ English shilling coin.

ṣìmṣìmṣìm Gossip.

ṣìsà-ɛ́kà Spread the (palm
of the) hand (to slap
someone).

ṣ̌ó Follow. Accompany.
Go with.

ṣ̌ó-ɔ́gwù̀ Inoculate; give
injection.

ṣ̌ònyí Queue up. Join a
line.

ṣ̌òtú-ɔ́k̃ú Tend fire by
rearranging or adding
more wood.

ṣ̌òtú Stoke (a fire).

sɔ (1) Avoid (out of
respect). Honour.
Revere. (2) Run
(away).

sɔ́ɓà Run into.

sɔ́ghá Abandon.

sɔ́ẖwùẖú Run and get lost.

sɔ́k̃úr̃ú Run up (a tree, hill
etc).

ṣ̌ɔ-óyi Be repulsive to see,
or touch; Abhor.
Disgust (of faeces or
dirty environment).

sɔ́pù̀rụ́ Worship and
respect.

sɔ̀táɦí   Run away.

sú   (Of war, or fight) start, or break out.

sùbá   Set or cock (a gun).

sụ̀gháryá   Boil. Begin to boil.

sụ́kwụ̀rụ́   Sit with knees drawn up.

sụ̀sụ̀rù   Tasteless.

sụ́swɔ́ɔ́   Be stupid.

sụ̀tà   Abundantly.

sụ̀tá   Chew hungrily.

sụ̀ụ́   (1) Speak (a language). (2) Pound (in a mortar).

s̃ụ̀ụ́   (1) Loss (in a business). (2) Stab. Pierce (with the end of a pointed object). (3) Cut. Clear (bush, grass, etc.)

s̃ụ́-úɗè   Grunt. Low groan.

swàá   (1) Wash (clothes). (2) Compress. Shorten. Be short or less.

s̃wàá   Cut, or mow (grass).

swɔ́ɔ́   (1) Jam. (2) End.

sh

shi   Smell. Stink. Give
scent.

shí   (1) Manifest. Show.
Appear (of the
moon). (2) Cook, as
in: Shí ŋdi *(cook
yam)*. (3) Set, as in:
Shí ɔ́nyà *(set a trap)*.

shìè   Cook; boil.

shìé   Smell.

shìé-íshì   Have odor, or
Smell.

shíghì-shìghí   Fumble
around; act blind.

shìhí   Become inured to
pain.

shìshì   A six-penny coin.

shìtá   (1) Cook (meat)
and eat. (2) Cook an
item until the water
dries.

shɔ́bú   Used to describe
skin covered with
rash etc.

t

ʈá   Blame.

ʈá   (Of water, or any liquid) drip.

ʈà   Now; Immediately.

tàá   Chew. Bite. Gnaw. Munch.

tàá   Dry up. Less (of liquid, flood, river etc).

tàá-íkìkére-éze   Gnash teeth. Grind molars together.

ʈàáni   Todav.

tàá-ŋcħařa   Rust, or become rusty.

tàá-ŋkarafɔŋ   Become rusty (Efik borrowing).

tàá-újárí   Rust, or corrode.

ʈàá-ǔʈa   Find fault, or blame.

ʈábùrù   (Used as the conditional) Before.

táʈúʈú   Suffer.

tágbwó   Bite to death.

tàħí-iꝄe   Be strong.

tàkásyá   (1) Squander (money) (2) Eat to pieces.

tákàyì   Whisper a conversation.

tàꝄétɔ   Adhere, or stick to.

tàꝄúřú   (Of burnt food, or glue) Stick to.

támù   Mutter. Murmur. Grumble.

tá-ŋcħařa   Be rusty.

tàpárì   Adhere, or stick to.

tàpyá   Crush with teeth.

tàpyá   (Slang) translate (foreign word).

tàrárá   (Become) clear.

ʈásàá   Drop a light sprinkle of water on.

tàwáá   Bite open.

tàwásì   (Of pain) Biting

tàwásyá   Bite to pieces

té   (1) Prepare (soup). (2) Rub. Smear. Paint.

ʈé   (1) Be flexible. Move in a flexible way (in dancing), as in ʈé írí *(dance),* and: ʈé ɔkpà *(walk with a limp).*

tèé-ófo   Prepare sauce, or soup.

ʈèħí   Wake up. Awake.

ʈé-írí   Dance.

ʈèlásá   Wake up in the middle of a sleep.

ʈé-ɔkpà   Limp, or walk with a limp.

térà-tèrá   Dance around (in joy).

tìró   Eve-lid make up. See **ɔtánjélé.**

tɔ   (1) Unwrap. Untie. Make naked. (2) To lay, place or spread (ears), as in Tɔ ŋcħì àlì *(listen very attentively).*

tɔ́-n̄wù "At your own time." <u>Used</u> as a form of greeting for somebody who has injured him (her) self or just working.

tɔ́ɒùú Loosen, or untie.

tɔ́rɔ́ English three-pence piece.

tɔ́rú̠ Untie and take an item tied with a rope.

tɔ́tɔ̀ntɔ́ Always wanting to eat all and everything.

tóolu Nine.

ʔú̠ Order. Request (somebody going to the market to help you buy something).

ʔú̠ (1) Extol. Salute by name. (2) Share.

tú State of being. Be affected, as in: Tú égw̃ù *(be afraid)*. Tú óyi *(be cold)*. Tú íme *(be pregnant)*.

ʔú̠-ɛ́ɾ̃à Extol the name, or salute by name; Hail.

ʔú̠-ɛ́jà Sacrifice something.

tú̠-n̄wòó Throw away, or discard.

tù̠lé Examine, or scrutinize closely.

tùghá Throw beyond, or past its mark.

tùgháryá Turn. Turn over.

tùgháryá-úchè Consider.

Reflect. Change mind.

tún̄wòó Throw away. Lose.

tù̠k̃úntu̠k̃ù̠ Hairy seed-pods of a plant with tiny hooks that tend to attach to human and animal skin.

túkwàsí Put or place on top.

túkwàsí-óbù Have hope on.

túkw̃ù̠r̃ú Squat; Go down on both knees.

tù̠-m̀kpɔ́rɔ́ Imprison or confine: Jail.

túnkɔ̀rínkɔ̀ Winding. Meandering.

tú̠-nwòó Change; exchange.

ʔù̠nyí Allocate; allot, or apportion.

tù̠pwó Open (a door, book etc).

ʔú̠sàá Distribute.

tù̠s̩í̃ɾ̃á (Of washed clothes) rinse.

tù̠rú̠ Lure away.

tù̠rú Be decked out (in a costume).

tù̠rú̠-íme Conceive.

tùtù Until. Till (Efik borrowing).

tù̠tú̠ Try out. Attempt.

tú̠tù̠kátá Pick together.

tú̠tù̠sá Pick up and bring.

tú̠tù̠sá Throw down.

tútútú Overestimation in counting.

tútútú Shaky.

tútwàá Gather. Pick up item by item.

tútwòó Scrub. Rub.

tùú (1) Measure. Measure to buy, as in: Tùú garri *(measure garri to buy)*. (2) Haul. Throw. (3) Just right. Enough (salt) to taste. (4) Carve. Sculpt. (5) Choke on.

tú-ùtù Dust, as a result of insect infestation.

tú-ùzù Be noisy. Make noise.

twàá Point (with the finger.

twàá-ègwà Be multicolored or spotted.

twàá-èkà (1). Point (a finger). (2) Show password to identify self as a member of a traditional secret society.

twàá-mbwɔ Pinch with the finger nails.

twàá-ŋtúbe Burrow, or dig a narrow tunnel.

twàá-óyi Make cool; cause to be cold.

twàá-ɔgù Make interpretable musical tunes playing on the wooden slit drum.

tw̃àá-ɔgw̃ù The act of being initiated into the traditional medicine profession.

twàá-ɔnu Give directions on how to get to a destination.

twàá-ínyìrì (Of cloth) be dirty.

twàá-íwu enact a law; issue an order, decree, legislate.

twàá-úr̃á Capable of inducing sleep.

twɔɔ Be sweet. Be in love. Be in good terms.

twɔɔ-ɔchị Be funny; capable of causing laughter.

twɔɔ-ùtwɔ Be Sweet, tasty, or pleasurable.

twòó Praise. Eulogize.

twòó Grow; Blossom.

twòrwòó Mature enough, or Be of age.

twòzwòó Old enough; b suitable, or of the right proportion.

u

ú In, At, as in: Ú'bì (*at the farm*).

úbì Farm.

úbi-ézi Back garden; farm around the homestead.

ùɓó A kind of native pear eaten after it had been softened in hot ash.

ùɓó-bèkéè Avocado pear.

ùɓóghìnì A kind of garden egg.

úɓómání A kind of vegetable leaves with purgative properties.

úbùbé Ladder.

úɓùɓò A kind of tree noted for its twisted and warped stem and branches.

Úbùrù A tribe noted for their occupation of making salt.

úche A kind of age grade retirement ceremony.

úchè Thought.

úchè-óba Traditional "yam barn watch" performed by young men as a step towards the formation of a viable age grade group in Amogudu.

úchè-ónyé-ani A contraption of sticks or (recently) cement the height of an adult built on farm routes that enables farmers load and offload their baskets without help.

úɗè Groan. Grunt.

ùɗé Reputation. Fame. Male name.

údé Raffia palm plantation.

ùdèlè Vulture.

ùdé-okoro Slang used to warn that an expression is "Not for real".

ùdíde Spider.

ùɗó Peace. Quietness. Calmness.

úɗò Sanity. Awareness of self, as in: Ényá úɗò (*of sound mind*).

ùdù Earthen ware pot with a hole in the neck used as a musical instrument.

ùdúdúru Damp, wet and rainy (weather).

ùdú-mini Rainy Season.

ùdú-ŋkɔlɔ A sharp blow to the neck with

the part of the hand
between the thumb
and the forefinger.

ùfé Flight.

úfòróyi Air. Breeze.

ùfùfé Wind.

úfúfye Reddish.

ùṛúfỹè Across.
Crosswise.

úfyé Camwood. Red
dye. Red.

ùfỹè Hollowed out
wooden drum

ùgèdú (used to describe
a person) Lazy; Slow
poke.

úghere Yawn.

ùg̃ò Eagle.

úgwú Hill. Mountain.

ùgw̃ù Respect.

úgw̃ù Circumcision.

úgwú-ɔ́kàgwó
Traditional ceremony
of the **Ègbóji**
community of
Ébíríbá.

úgwúṛíṛi Refuse dump.

úñére Willingness.
Zeal.

újíri Orange.

újíri-ɛ́ghíríghá
Trifoliate orange
usually very bitter
and not edible fresh.

újíri-ɔ̀gw̃ù̀-ŋ́ma Lemon.

ùkè (1) Age grade. (2)
A kind of evil spirit
said to afflict

children with terrible
conditions like the
loss of the front teeth
etc.

ùkébè Enema. (Efik
borrowing).

ùkéji-àgbàlà The
principal
administrative age
grade responsible for
executing the laws
enacting by the **ézè**
at a particular time in
Ébíríbá.

ùkòghò Any contraption
for storing dried corn.

ùkpékw̃ù Back of the
head.

ùkpóghudà Bamboo.

Ùkpó One of the
subdivisions of
Ám̃éK̃e in **Ébíríbá**
comprising of **Í̧dé**
Agwu, **Í̧dé Ńko, Í̧dé**
Owòm, **Í̧dé** Oɡbe,
and Ukpó Agbɔ̀.

úkpò A kind of cotton
printed wrapper cloth.

ùkpó-òrò A kind of
large edible garden
egg usually eaten raw.

ùkpótùmà Fresh beans
not yet dry enough to
harvest.

ùkùghùkúghu Owl.

ùK̃úK̃ùṛú-úlwò Thatch
roof.

úkùrútù Cannon.

ùkw̃òmìnì A kind of
    edible clay.
ùkw̃ù Bundle.
úkw̃ù Waist.
úkw̃u-ɔ̀k̃àr̃à Piece of
    wrap fabric of about
    forty-five inches
    wide and six yards
    long.
úkw̃ù-ósísí The base of
    a tree.
úlwò House.
úlwò-ɛ́kw̃a Traditional
    wake-keeping.
úlwò-ɛ́kwúkwɔ́ School.
úlwò-élu Storey
    building.
úlwò-ikwu Membership
    of the traditional
    maternal extended
    family.
úlwò-ŋ́kwụ Huts built
    along farm routes
    where weary farmers
    can rest.
úlwò-ńnɔ Latrine.
úlwò-ńtà Main building.
úlwò-ɔ̀fya *(A kind of
    wild leaves cooked to
    produce a slimy
    gruel used as)* Mud
    Floor paint
    producing a dark
    green patina for
    keeping dust away,
    and for decoration.
úlwò-ɔ̀gwu *(Medicine
    house)* Hospital;

place for the care of
    the sick.
úlwò-ɔ̀k̃àr̃à Traditional
    cloth hut used mostly
    for weddings and
    úche ceremonies
úm̃ó Breathe. Strength.
ùnà Three-leafed yam,
    usually yellowish in
    color.
ùnè Banana.
únù You; yours (plural).
ùnùghùnúghù-ɔ̀kpù
    Haemorrhoids. Piles.
ùnyó (1) Baboon. (2)
    A kind of children's
    disease characterized
    by the appearance of
    large boils on the
    patient's body.
úpòghúpò Name given
    to a kind of insect
    with large wings and
    a tiny body.
úre Corruption. Rot.
    Decomposition.
úrè Dance of joy.
ùrékpù Plant with
    leaves producing a
    kind of medicinal sap
    used as an antiseptic.
ùrézè Cotton wool.
ùrí-ɔ̀k̃u Dried palm fruit
    stigma soaked in oil
    grease and used as a
    lighter.
úróm Bottle.
úrù Profit. Advantage.

úrùghúrù Succulent, juicy part.

ùrúmakw̃ù A kind of snake.

ùrwóɗá Almost round, thick underground medicinal stem, heated and applied on the skin on top of a fractured bone to expedite healing.

ùryè A kind of plant with fruits which when ground, produce indigo dye used for marking tattoos on the body.

úšo A widow's period of mourning at which she is not allowed to associate with the other members of the society.

ùšókw̃u Traditional kitchen.

úté Mat.

úžú Dust.

ụ

ụ̀bá   Plentiful; Wealth; Increase; Prosperity; an increase in size.

ụ̀bára   A continuous series or flow, as in: Ụ̀bára-ɛ́h|úhú *(a stream of ants)*.

ụ́bụ́bá   (1) A kind of mushroom. (2) A kind of tree.

ụ́bụ̀bwɔ́   Story; Tale; Narrative.

ụ̀búrụ̀   Brain.

ụ̀bụ̀rụ̀   A yellow succulent sweet-smelling edible fruit with a tangy taste and a tendency to sensitize the teeth.

ụ́bwɔchǐ   Day.

ụ̀bwɔló   Shrubs.

ụ́byá   See ụ́byáŋgo.

ụ̀byá   An arrival.

ụ̀byǎ   The act of gaining an unfair advantage by trickery; Cheat

ụ́byáŋgo   A kind of tree: its wood having a soft pith and noted for making crackling and explosive sounds when burning.

ụ̀byàm   State of hardship, or want; indigence.

Ụ̀chá   Female name.

ụ̀chá   Cleanliness; whiteness.

ụ̀chụ̀   An unseen force, a person, or something such as a curse that is thought to bring bad luck.

ụ́dà   A kind of tree with strong smelling fruits used as an ingredient in the preparation of various medicine and in certain dishes.

ụ́dà   Sound. Report.

ụ́dà-égbè   Sound of a gun shot.

Udàńtà   One of the subdivisions of Ámógùdù in Ɛ́bíríbá comprising of Ńdé Okoronkwo, Ŋ́dé Mbã-ɔ̀gū, Agbɔ́-úka, Ŋ́dé Okᴘóto. Ŋ́dé Nwébà, Ŋ́dé Ɔ́nwúka-úzo-úbì, and Umuobworo which is subdivided into Ŋ́dé Eià. Ŋ́dé Ewúrezi, and Ŋ́dé Okóró Ụ̀kpabi.

ụ́dárà   African star apple.

ụ́dárà-ɛ̀bwɔ́   A temporary place of settlement by the Ɛ́bíríbá people around the present Okagwe and Elu in Ohafya.

ụ̀dɔ́   Rope. Cord.

ùdị̀ Type or kind.

ùdwɔ́ A general scramble, or ruch to grab, or snatch something.

ùfighị̀-úfị Twisted tangle.

ùfɔ́dị̀ Some; a few.

ùfúfa A kind of large bird

ùfyɔ́ Quarrel

ùgá Path.

ùgá-mang Acrobatics.

ùgárá Foot path.

ùgbá Dish of sliced cooked oil-bean prepared with spices and cooked cow hide in the form of a salad.

ùgbághá Oil bean seed usually dispersed by explosive mechanism.

úgbàlà Duck.

úgbɔ́ Vehicle, Vessel, or craft like Canoe, Boat, Ship, Car, Plane etc.

úgbɔ́-ali Car; Lorry; Trucks; Van.

úgbɔ́-élu Airplane.

úgbɔ́-éja Wooden board used for holding sacrificial items.

úgbɔ́-épépé Dug out canoe.

úgbɔ̀ghɔ̀ Vegetable leaves.

úgbɔ̀ghɔ̀-ɛ̀múmà Plant of the squash family *(Cucurbita pepo)* whose leaves are used for vegetable gumbo, and the seeds used for food preparation.

úgbɔ̀ghɔ̀-ùrù Wild vegetable.

úgbɔ́-mini Ship: Boat.

úgbɔ́-ḿbwɔ́ghɔ́rɔ́ Wooden board serving as cutting surface.

úgbɔ́ nwánkpi A traditional form of leave-township in which an employee or apprentice in a sojourning town is sent back to the village as a form of punishment usually for committing a crime.

ùgbú Fishing net.

ùgbú Masquerade costumes, (usually made with netting.

úgbúgbɔ̀ Bark of the trunks, boughs and branches of trees usually medicial. Another name for talisman.

ùghá Falsehod. Lie.

ùghàlà Repeated performance of (trade etc).

úg̃u (See ɛ́kwúkwɔ́-óf̃i)

úgùrù Harmattan.

úgwà Eczema.

úgwá Redemption.

úgwɔ Debt. Wages. Salary.

úgwɔ-ɔ́nwa Monthly salary.

úr̃wɔ́ Remainder, or
what's leftover.

úr̃wú Peppery hot; pain

ùjàrà Dancing rattle-bead
made by stringing cut
pieces of the shells of
dried seeds, or nuts and
usually tied around the
ankle to sound in time
with the dancer's
moves.

újárí Decaying. Rusting
(of metal or iron).

úka Sourness (of soup
gone bad); become
rancid.

úkà Talk. Argument.
Disputation.

úkabì Farmland in which
only the yam tubers
have been harvested.

ùkárá Dark blue wrapper
with white drawings of
reptiles worn by
initiated men, mostly
for traditional
ceremonies and ékpè
society outings. (Efik
borrowing).

ùkàtázu Happening in
your absence, or after
you have gone.

ùkàtùrù Too strong (of
vegetable pass its prime)
to use.

ùkɔ́ Scarcity. Want.

ùkɔ́r̃u Bamboo or wood
shelving in traditional
kitchens.

úkɔ́m Plantain (Efik
borrowing)

úkpa Inability to resist
(food).

ùkpákà A traditional
dance with a grotesque
mask (Efik borrowing).

ùkpálughujì Castanets
made of tennis ball-
sized gourds.

ùkpátá Idol. Small statue.

ùkpázùghùzù A kind of
red succulent fruit.

ùkpírìkpɔ̀ Yam seedlings.

ùkpɔ́ A kind of small,
bitter áŋàr̃à used
mainly for preparing
sauce for eating yam.

ùkpɔ́-ɛ́kà Cracking the
knuckles.

ùkpɔ́kwừrừ Sun-dried cut
up okra.

ùkpɔ̀rɔ̀fífì Whistle.

ùkpɔ̀mỹr̃ĩnkĩchỹ Flying
termite.

úkừ Dance (now defunct)
by Úmùɔ́bwɔrɔ̀ women
characterized by the
stamping of feet.

úkwárà Cough.

úkwárà-ŋ̀kélu Whooping
cough..

úkwárà-ŋ́tà Tuberculosis.

úkwárà-ùnú-èbùlù
Asthma

úkwú Leg. Foot.
Footsteps.

ùkw̃úkw̃a Fruit resembling mango the seed of which is used cooking ingredient.

ùlá Departure. Going home.

ùlàrì Silken decorative item.

úlɔ̀gbɔ̀ Disc beads worn around the waist by nubile girls.

ùmà Behaviour. Attitude.

ùm̃à Extra, or left over after a set quantity is accounted for.

úmɔ́n Name of place town in the upper cross river where Abiriba sojourned. The name is now used to describe those who sojourned in the areas stretching from Umon down the Cross River to the borders of Cameroon by the Atlantic ocean.

úmù̀ See úmúr̃ìmá.

Úmúes̃ò One of the subdivisions of Ám̃ék̃e comprising Ŋ́dé Ùwéka, Ŋ́dé Okórye. Ŋ́dé Ɔ̀tá, Ŋ́dé Ukpo, Ŋ́dé Anúkú. Ŋ́dé Ùtúbi-Agbɔ̀. Ŋ́dé Ɔ́ku, Ŋ́dé Ekpè, Ŋ́dé Egbòó, Ŋ́dé Orírí, Ŋ́dé Mbã-ɛkũ, Ŋ́dé Akoo, Ŋ́dé Ezèmá, Ŋ́dé Akwú, Ŋ́dé Nkwokõcha, Kìrĩ̀,

and Ŋ́dé Ùtúbị-elu.

Úmúechúkú One of the subdivisions of Ám̃ógùdù in Ɛ́bíríbá comprising of Ŋ́dé Ɛ́gwū, Ŋ́dé Ùbàm, Ŋ́dé Elefõ-ágbɔ̀. Ŋ́dé Okóchã, Ŋ́dé e'Mang, Ŋ́dé Ogõ, Ŋ́dé Elefõ-elu, Ŋ́dé Ɔ́nwuka, Ŋ́dé Ɛ́jà.

úmúnnà Kinsmen usually of the same compound.

úmú-ɔ́kwùrù̀ Kingmakers responsible for the nomination, or selection of an incoming head of a village.

úmúr̃ìmá Children.

ùnà Species of yam *(dioscorea dumetorum Pax)* with three-pronged leaved.

ùná Trouble.

úŋàr̃à Feeling damp and sweaty.

úŋàr̃à A situation capable of inducing sweat.

únwụ A period of scarcity of food.

ùnvàn̄i Yesterday.

úr̃á Sleep.

úr̃á-ŋ́tà Sleeping sickness.

ùrághá (1) Smooth and shiny. (2) Bald, as in: Ísí ùrághá *(bald-headed)*.

ùrághá Large smooth

stone used for mud wall smoothening and plastering.

úráyịkáng Matches (Efik borrowing).

úrị Wandering.

ùrịghị Sneaky disappearance; dodge.

úrɔ̀ Joy.

ùrɔ́ Usually a dance (of shame) in which a thief is made to dance around the market or village with the stolen ware.

ùrú Wickedness. Mischief.

úr̃ù A kind of tree.

ùrùrɔ̀ Mud.

ùsàn Plate (Efik borrowing).

ùsárị Traditional dance of the Ám̃ógùdù people.

ùsháká Dried pod of okra etc., containing dried seeds that rattle when shaken.

ùshághúshá A kind of dried fruit with a strong smell and taste used as a medicinal and soup condiment.

úsú Bat.

Ụsúmani A popular stream in Ám̃ógùdù.

ùsùswɔ̀ The end.

ùswɔ̀tù End.

úta Blame. Reprimand.

útá Bow.

útàŋ-ɛ̀sɛ̀ Traditional dance performed by members of the Ulwo Uku. (Efik borrowing).

útá-ŋgw̃ùr̃ù Cramps. Numbness of part of the body.

útàr̃à Any pounded food taken with soup or sauce.

útàr̃à-íkpákpà Pounded corn meal.

útàr̃à-ŋ́di Pounded yam meal.

útàr̃à-íwa Pounded cassava meal.

ùtàzù A spicy kind of bitter vegetable leave used in soup.

ùtɔ́rɔ̀ Brain, or bone marrow.

ùtɔ̀rɔ̀ñwúñwù Foam. Froth.

ùtù A kind of orange-red sweet flesh fruit growing on a thick bush.

ùtù A weevil or other kinds of tiny beetles that attack and destroy trees, nuts, grains, and fruits by boring into them; whitish powder produced by the weevil or other insects.

útụ Money, or kind paid as tax, collection, rent, fee etc.

ụ́tụ́-ɛ́fa Sandy clay.
ụ̀tụ́kà Place beyond; on the other side.
ụ̀tụ́rùkátá Perplexed.
ụ́tụ̀rụ́kpà A kind of tree with leaves that look like those of the óko tree and sometimes used in place of óko leaves.
ụ̀tụ́tụ́ Morning. Early in life.
ụ̀tụ́tụ́-ɔ́má (A direct translation for the greeting) Good Morning.
ụ̀twɔ́ Sweetness; tasty; pleasure.
ụ̀wà World; Universe; Destiny.
ụ̀wà Piece cloth wound around the waist and passing between the legs to be tied in place in the back.
ụ̀wàsi Sickness; a state of being ill. Suffering from an ailment.
ụ́ʐ̣ịzá Tiny, black medicinal pepper used as a spice.
ụ́zɔ̀ Way. Road. Path. Door.
ụ́zɔ̀-íyi Tradition festival characterized by young women engaging in an exchange of insult with other young women in out door repartee.
ụ́zɔ̀-ɔ́fya Short cut bush road.
ụ́ʐ̃ụ́ (1) Blacksmithing. (2) Place of sojourn.
ụ̀ʐ̃ụ̀ Noise. Uproar. Quarrel.

V

váa Exremely bright, as
in: Nwú váa *(shine
brightly)*.

vàm Used to describe:
Swift and suddenly.

vàráŋgídì Blanket.
(English borrowing).

vúù-vúu Being blown
this way and that.

W

wá Them. Their.

wà Cut, as in: Wà ŋdi *(cut yam)*. Split. Divide. Space.

wàá Break. Shatter (of bottles and breakables).

wàá-àlị Demarcate land boundaries, or plots.

wàá-ɛnyà Be assertive, bold.

wàá-niàkpà Forked.

wàá-ɔ́ji Break kola nut.

wàá-ólìlyè Storm off (in anger).

wàpwó Make a hole by piercing with a sharp, pointed object.

wábàá Push into with force.

wàrà-wàrà Narrow.

wàrɛnyà 'Be strong', More grease to your

wụ̀á Bathe.

wụ̀á-ħwú Take a bath.

wúħwòó Pour away, or spill.

wùrí Cook for self.

elbows etc., (used to encourage somebody engaged in a task).

wàsá Subpoena visit by a traditional secret society like ɔ̀bɔ̀n etc., to litigants.

wàyí Insert. Put in between too close a place or object with little or no space between them.

wóɗà Climb down.

wòghátá Roll around.

wòó (1) Be angry. Annoyed. (2) Roll.

wɔ̀ɔ́ Refuse to give.

wɔ̀ŋḳîṛîwɔ̀ Wood shavings from a carpenter's workshop.

wɔ́wɔ̀ɔ́ Shrub with razor-sharp stems and leaves.

wùú (1) Pain. (2) Cook.

wụ̀ú (1) Bathe. (2) Pour. (3) Buy (crayfish, groundnut, kernel, okra).

y

y' Including. With. And. as in: Ébìtú y' Ɛ́nyá *(Ebitu and Ɛnya)*.

yá <u>Reflective</u> It/ Him/ Her, as in: Kèlé yá *(greet him/her)*.

yàá Sieve.

yà-me Therefore; It so happens.

yèé Put. Add.

yèé-Ɛkà Help; assist; give a helping hand.

yèé-ɔ̀Ƙu Set a fire, or torch.

yéghé-yéghé (Of river, stream,) being sparkling clean.

yéghé-yèghè-yéghé (Treat wrong by giving a person) the run around.

yóo (1) Him/Her/It. (2) He/She.

yɔ̀ghɔ́ríyɔ̀ One of the many masquerades of the Ɛ́bịrịbá Béndè festooned with ékpiri.

Z

zàá (1) Answer or reply to a call. (2) Become less (in quantity or height). (3) Swell (of welt). (4) Filter. Skim off. (5) Sweep.

zèñí Dissolve, as in: Gbázèñí *(melt)*.

zèé Dodge. Shrink from. Avoid.

ẑèé Collapse (of building or structure).

ẑèé Fall sick (of a person).

ẑèé The act of throwing something, or somebody to the ground.

ẑèé-úm̃ò Die (take a last breath).

zèérí Avoid; stay away from.

ẑí Teach. Instruct. Show.

ẑìñá-ímì Blow the nose

ẑìí Blow (the nose).

ẑí-ŋdùghú Sneeze.

zìsá Send down.

zìsár̨m Send down to me.

ẑízèñi (Of food) completely digested so that one feels hungry again.

zɔgbwó Trample to death.

ẑɔñú (Of a married woman) leave a matrimonial home.

zɔɔ́ Step on.

zɔɔ́ Forget.

zɔpyá Smash or crush underfoot

zúkɔɔ́ Meet, or gather.

ẑừrú Steal.

zừú (1) Buy. (2) Clean undigested food from the intestines of an animal.

zùú Complete. Enough. Accurate.

ẑùú Humming low dronning noise.

zúzùú Be stupid.

zúzwàá Scrub (a floor with dyes).

zwàá Buy.

ẑwàá Train. Nurture.

zwóñwòó Conceal, or hide something to a point of losing it.

zwòó Hide.

zwòó Be enough.

ẑwòó Steal.

zyèé Report to, or inform.

ẑỹèé Put down (a load).

Part II
English-Abiriba

a

Abandon ghàá
Abandon sɔ́ghá
Abdominal tumor ɔ́bà-
ɛ́ẁwɔ
Aberration áru
Abomination áru
Abomination ĩ́ẃénsɔ
Abomination ŋ́sɔ́
About ébé
About gbásá
Abscess ónwo
Abscond ẁèʈáẁí
Absent ánɔ̀ghù
Absent ábyaghị̀-abya
Absorb mị́
Abundantlv sụ̀tà
Abuse kɔ́-ɔnu
Accede kwòó
Accept náẁàsá
Accessories ɛ́kwásí
Accident ɔ̀ghɔ́m
Accident prone m̀gbà̱m
Accompany ʃ́ó
Accompany dùú
Accurate zùú
Accuse bwó
Ache ẁwụ̀ụ́-ụ̀ẁwú
Achilles tendon áꞮù-ɔ́kpà
Acrobatics ụ̀gá-mang
Across ùꞮúfȳ̀è
Act òmùmé
Action òmùmé
Acuteness ŋ́kɔ́
Adage ílu
Adam's apple ɛ́kpù-ǹkɔ́lɔ̀

Add yèé
Add up g̃ụ̀kátá
Adder ɛ́ɓụ́-àẁ̀
Adhere tàꞭétɔ́
Adhere tàpárị́
Adhere to nyànꝺé
Adjudicate kɒè-íkpe
Admission ŋ́naɓàsá
Admit náɓàsá
Adolescent boy òkóró-
ɔ̀byà
Adult ónyé-ìchȳ̀è
Advantage úrù
Advice ɔ́ꝺụ
Advice ǹꝺùmɔ́ꝺù
Advice dɔ̀ɔ́-ɛká-ńcẁ̀
Afar ényá-ènyà
Africa Áfìríkà
After émé
Afternoon ò g̃èꝶé
Afterwards éméẁá
Agape gbàghébé
Age grade ùkè
Age mates ébúrú
Aged óchȳ̀è
Agree kwòó
Agreement òkwúkwó
Ahead íẁw̃ú
Ailment èlwà
Air úfòróyi
Airplane úgbɔ́-élu
Albino bèkéè-hwú úzɔ̀ lwá
ìgbò
Algae èkpétu
Alien land m̀bà

Alike díbyà
Alive ŋ̃dù
All òzùgbà
Alligator pepper óšò-ŋ̃si
Allocate ʈùnyí
Allot ʈùnyí
Allotment òkè
Almighty ɔ̀kákáà
Alone ani
Alphabet ábígbí
Alteration ŋ́gḇanwò
Ambush chèčínyé
Amicable bwághá-bwághá
Among íme
Amulet éK̃íK̃é
Ancient óchỹè
Angel mó'zi
Anger íwó
Angle ŋ́kɔ́
Animal ánú
Animal ánụ̀-mànù
Ankle ákpụ̀rákpụ̀
Announce sàyí
Annoyed wòó
Another ɔ̀dwɔ́
Answer zàá
Answer ɔ̀sìsà
Ant éẽ́ụ̃̃́ụ̃́
Antelope élé
Anthill ìkúbe
Anthill ŋ́kɒú
Antidote ŋ́tárụ́
Antidote ɔ́fà
Anus íK̃è
Anus òtùlà
Anus ɔ̀nyụ́nyụ́-ŋ̀ší
Apart ákwà
Ape àdáka

Apex ŋ́nụ́nụ
Apology èghórò
Appeal èghórò
Appear shí
Appear bwɔ́
Appear pụ̀sá
Appease gwàá
Appendicitis ɔ́gbá-kpụ́rụ̀rụ̀
Apportion ʈùnyí
Apprentice nwántà-ụ́žụ̀
Arena ɔ̀gbɔ́
Argue rụ̀tá
Argument ụ́kà
Arm ɛ́ká
Armament ŋ́gwá-ágha
Armed robbers
àbàlìdìmégw̃ù
Armpit ɛ́ɓụ̀
Around gbùrùgbúrù
Around gbùrù-gbúrù
Arrange čòbé
Arrest ŋ́K̃eři
Arrest K̃èr̃ì
Arrogant nyàá-ísi
Arrow ákú
Art ŋ̀kà
Arthritis ŋ̀jìghínjì
Artificial àdígbòlója
Artist òménkà
As ìlèghè
Ash ŋ̃ʈú
Ashy ŋ́tụ́ŋ̀tụ̀
Aside ákwà
Ask jụ̀
Assent òkwúkwó
Assets èK̃ụ̀
Assist yèé-ɛ́kà

Asthma ʊ́kwárà-ùnú-
èbùlù
Astonish jù-ényá
At é
At á as in: Á'fyá (at the
market).
At first è'm̀bú
Ate rì
Athlete's foot ídìdè
Atrophy kpɔ̀nw̃úá
Attempt tùtú
Attire ŋ́gwá
Attitude ʊ̀mà

Audacious kàɦágbà
Authentic ézíya
Authority íƙé
Average ègbàtà
Avocado pear ùɓó-bèkéè
Avoid sɔ
Avoid zèé
Avoid zèérí
Avoidance ŋ́sɔ́
Awake ìèɦí
Awaken kpɔ̌é
Awkward m̀bɪ́rɪ́
Ax ényʊ́nƙu

b

Baboon ùnyó
Baby nwɔ́ɦwúr̃u
Bachelor óƙé-òkpòrò
Back àžú
Back door ɪ̀zɔ́fɔ̀rɔ̀
Back yard ɪ̀zɔ́fɔ̀rɔ̀
Back-bite kpàkásyá
Bad ɔ́íɔ́ɔ
Bad jɔ́
Bad luck iɦw̃ú-ɔ́íɔ́ɔ
Bad thing ɪ́ɪ̃́fé-ɔ́jɔ́ɔ
Badness ŋ́jó
Baffled ɡbàkwʊ́r̃ʊ́
Bag èkpà
Baggage íbú
Balance ɪ̀ɦàtíɦà
Bald ísí-ŋkwɔ́cɦá
Bald ŋ́kwɔ́cɦá
Bamboo ùkpóghudà

Bamboo shelving ʊ̀kɔ́ƙu
Banana ùnè
Barber ɔ̀kɒú-íshí
Bareness ɔ̀tɔ́
Bark (of a dog) gbɔ̀ɔ́
Barrel ábán
Base ɔ̀kpù
Baske nyàá
Bat ʊ́sʊ́
Bathe wʊ̀ʊ́
Bathe wʊ̀á
Be bʊ̀
Be dì
Be angry wòó
Be burnt r̃èé
Be enough zwòó
Be lost ɦw̃ùɦú
Be loyal rùbé-ísí
Be rich bá

Be strong tàh̃í-ik̃e
Be wealthy bá
Beach ɔ́nú-ésụ
Beach umbrella àwàkísɔ̀ng
Beans àgwà
Bear bùú
Beard ẽjí-àgbà
Beast ánú
Beast ánụ̀-mànụ̀
Beautiful òvóvò
Beautiful ɔ́má
Beauty ńma
Beauty ị̃di-ŋ́ma
Because màkà
Because níh̃ì
Bed óji
Bedbugs èkpị̀rị̀
Bed-room m̀kpúrù
Bee   éŋu
Beef ánụ̀-námà
Beetle àkpàghàrà
Before ɛ̀'m̀bú
Before ìábụ̀rụ̀
Beg ryɔ́
Beget mù
Begging árị̀ryɔ́
Begging èghórò
Beginner ìtì
Behaviour ụ̀mà
Behaviour émùmé
Behaviour ègwà
Belch ŋ̀kɔ̀
Bell átáŋ
Bellows ék̃ò
Belly éh̃wɔ́
Belt ãj̃ì
Bench óché

Bend (down) k̃wùú
Beneath òkpúrù
Bent gbèé
Bent gbéghàtá
Bent ńgbéré
Bent ŋ̀kɔ̀gbé
Bequeath nwúghà
Bereft ŋ́kwɔ́ch̃á
Berth dùyí
Bet m̃àr̃í-ɛ́kà
Betrayal m̀gbá-òkpúrù
Beware kɒàch̃ár̃í-énya
Bicycle ɔ̀kpɔ́ɔ̀
Bicycle ánàghúkwà
Bicycle ígwò
Big àyàwùrù
Big ók̃é
Big àg̃àgh̃àr̃à
Big toe ézè-ɔ́kpà
Bigness ókpù
Bind fyé
Binding ɛ́gbụ́
Bird ŋ́nụ̀nụ̀
Birthmark m̀bùm-pụ̀sá-ụ̀wà
Biscuit èchịch̃àr̃à
Bite ér̃ụ́
Bite tàá
Bite to death tágbwó
Bitter òlígbù
Bitter ílú
Black ójíi
Blackness ŋ̀jíí
Blacksmith ɔ̀kpụ̀-ụ̀z̃ụ̀
Blacksmithery kpwàá-ụ́zụ́
Blacksmithing ụ́z̃ụ́
Bladder èkpà-mámiri
Blame ìàá-ụ́ìa

Blame ɓá
Blame ụ̃ta
Blanket vàráŋgídì
Bleed gbàá-menyi
Bless gɔ̀zvé
Blessing ŋ́gɔ́zí
Blindness ìshì
Blindness ényámkpɔ́
Block cħí
Blockage òcħícħí
Blocked chỹé
Blood ményi
Bloody ményi-ményi
Blossom twòó
Blow kụ́
Blow kù
Blow (air) ħwụ̀ụ́
Blow (off) ħwụ̀pụ̀ụ́
Blunder ríkèé
Boast kpá-ŋ̃ã̀nã̀
Boast ɓá
Boat ụ́gbɔ́-mini
Body ħwú
Boil sùgháryá
Boil gbɔ̀ɔ́
Boil ónwo
Boil shìé
Boisterous bwághá-
bwághá
Bold wàá-ényà
Bold ɔ̃̀ĩ̃r̃ĩ̃ã̀-ényà
Boldness ényá-íke
Bolt (a door) gbàchỹé
Bond ɛ́gbú
Bone ɔ́kpúkpú
Bone marrow ùtɔ́rɔ̀
Book ɛ́kwụ́kwɔ́
Border òkè-àl̃ị

Borrow gbàʒ́írí
Borrow ŋ̀ụ̀r̃ú
Borrowing ǹʒ́íʒ́í
Borrowing ŋ̀ŋ̀ụ̀nụ̀
Boss ónvé-ísí
Boss ŋ́nà-úkú
Bottle ékpém
Bottle úróm
Bottom òkɒúrù
Bottom ɔ̀kpù
Bottom ír̃è
Boundary ɛ̀gbàtà
Boundary ókè
Boundary òkè-àl̃ị
Bow ụ́tá
Bowl àgbàngbà
Bowl ɔ́kwá
Box ìgbé
Boxing ógbón
Boy nwántà-ụ́ʒ̀ụ̀
Boy nwókoro
Boy òkóró
Bracelet m̀gbàréká
Braid kpàá
Brain ụ̀búrù
Brain ụ̀tɔ́rɔ̀
Branch (of a tree) ɛ̀pá
Branches (of a cut tree)
ɛ̀wɔ̀rɔ̀
Brassieres ŋ́kóróbá
Brazen ɔ̃̀ĩ̃r̃ĩ̃ã̀-ényà
Bread ɛ̀chị̀cħàr̃à
Break nyábwòó
Break jì
Break kèwá
Break kùwá
Break lɔ̀wàá
Break nyàjyé

Break wàá
Break gbàjyé
Break (of day) bwɔ́ɔ́
Break kola nut wàá-ɔ́ji
Break off nvájìpų́
Breasts ɛ́r̃á
Breath m̃ó
Breathe úm̃ó
Breeze úfòróyi
Bribe ŋ̀gàrì
Brief m̀bų̀bà
Bright nwú
Brim ójó-ɔ́nu
Bring gwòsá
Broad òɒòtóró
Broad ɔ̀sị̀sá
Broad àbàdábà
Broil ñw̃àá
Broom ɛ́zízà
Brow ókpóró-íñw̃u
Bruise áru
Bucket pánị̀
Buck-tooth éze-ògóm
Buffalo ãt̃ų́
Bug ŋ̀là
Bull ɛ́r̃í
Bull òkè-ɛ́r̃i
Bull's eye ényáya
Bullets m̀gbɔ
Bump dú
Bunch ɔ́yɔ̀ghų̀yɔ̀
Bundle ùkw̃ù

Bundle ŋ́gw̃ùgw̃ù
Burden íbú
Burdensome nyìí
Burial òlìlì
Burn ịkpɔ-ɔ́k̃ù
Burn ñùú
Burp ŋ̀kɔ̀
Burrow twàá-ŋ́túbe
Bury lìbé
Bury lí
Bush ɔ́fyá
Bush m̀gbóko
Bush meat ánú-ɔ́fva
Bush rat òké-ɔ́fya
Business capital ísí-
òkpòghò
But ɔ́bų
Butterfly èrèkèrè-m̀búba
Buttocks ɔ̀kpù
Buttocks ápị̀rị̀pá-ɔ̀kpù
Buttocks ík̃è
Buttocks òtùlà
Buxom pòghò-pòghò
Buy wų̀ų́
Buy zų̀ų́
Buy g̃òó
Buy kwá
Buy zwàá
Buy lú
Buy (hoe, matchet) gbàá
Bye gàní
By-pass m̃àfé

172

c

Calabash òɓò
Calabash àgbɔ̀
Calabash ɔ́bà
Calculate g̃úkɔ́tá
Calf ḿbùghúnè
Calico ábáčá.
Call kɒɔ̀t̨ú
Call kpɔ́-òkù
Call òkù
Callus ótùtù
Calm jàyì
Calm jùn̄ú
Calmness ùɗó
Camphor ɔ́gw̃ù-ékw̃u
Camwood úfyé
Can ògb̠óŋ
Cancel kàgbwó
Cane m̀kpá
Cane áŋa
Canned fish chánìvà
Canned-fish áʒ̃ù-cháŋ̀
Cannon úkùrútù
Cap òkpú
Capacious ògbú
Capsize kpùú
Capture kpà-ághá
Car ụ́gbɔ́-ali
Carcass óʒ̃ú
Cargo íbú
Carry bùrú
Carry bùú
Carry kwɔ́
Carry pàá
Carry across pághà
Carry around pàgháryá

Carry away pàpụ́ụ̀
Carry home pàlá
Carry into páɓà
Carry off búpụ̀
Carrying òbúbú
Carve pį̃
Carve íkpu
Carve tụ̀ụ́
Carved wooden image
ér̃únsị-áp̃ìr̃àp̃í
Casket ìgbé-óʒ̃ù
Cassava ị̀wá
Cassava farm ɔ̀bụ́bwɔ́-
ị̀wa
Cassava stem ókpèrè-ị̀wa
Castrate òkìrì
Catarrh ímí-ómúmé
Catch ɓànɗé
Catch ghɔ̀ɔ́
Catch kw̃ú
Catch nwụ̀r̃ụ́
Catfish àrírá
Cemetery òlìlì-óʒ̃ú
Center èchìchì
Centipede ɔ̀tàgbùlàghì-
nɔ́mɔghɔ̀
Centipede álị̀là
Chaff échàghàrì
Chain m̀kpɔ́rɔ́
Chains ókpórìmá
Chair óché
Chamber pot pòó
Chameleon ógùmágàlà
Champion wrestler
dímgba

Chance éfè
Chance òpété
Change gbánwò
Change ghɔ́ɔ́
Change mègháryá
Change ńgbanwò
Change tú-nwòó
Change color chàgháryá
Charcoal ínyĩ̀rĩ̀
Charm ɔ́gw̃ù
Chase chwàá
Chase chụ-ɔ́sɔ́
Chase off chụ-pụ
Cheap ɛ́ká-ɛ́mụ̀mà
Cheap ɔ̀nyụ́pà
Cheap price ɔ́nu-ɔma
Cheat ghɔ̀gbwó
Cheat ghɔ́ɔ́
Cheat kpàtá-ényà
Cheat kpá-ụ̀bỹà
Checkers èpèlé
Cheek ágbáǹchì̃
Cheek ásã́
Chest óbù
Chew tàá
Chewing stick étụ́
Child nwá
Child birth ɔ̀mùmú
Children úmụ́rĩ̀má
Chill óyi
Chisel átú
Choke kpàgbwó
Choke on tụ̀ú
Cholera nvúr̃ụ́-gbɔ́rú
Choose h̃ɔ́ɔ́
Church ịkɔ̀bàsì
Circle gbùrùgbúrù
Circumcision úgw̃ù

Civilization ĩ̀fè
Clamp kpàndé
Clamp shut kpàchỹé
Clams ákị̃rĩ̀syà
Clap kú
Clay ɔ́rwá
Clay pot ìtè-òtù
Cleanliness ụ̀chã́
Clear s̃ùú
Clever àkɔ́
Cliff ɔ́h̃w̃u
Climb nyìí
Climb down wóɗà
Climb onto nyìk̃úr̃ú
Climbing plant gbágbalì
Climbing rope ágbú -nkwú
Cling on k̃ụ̀ndé
Clitoris ã̀tùtù
Clock átáŋ
Close mèchỹé
Close ǹswó
Close fitting fá-ŋfagha
Cloth àbàdá
Cloth ńwéví
Clothing ńgwá
Clutch kpákwụ̀rụ́
Coal tar kòròtá
Cob ìshíshì
Cobwebs ǹg̃ùg̃úr̃u-úde
Cock ók̃é-ɔ̀kúkụ̀
Cock-eyed ényà-mgbélú-
óko
Cockroach ɔ̀chị̃cha
Coconut ák̃í-bèkeé
Cocoyam ǹkàsị́
Cocoyam leaves ópòtó-
ǹkàsì
Coffin ìgbé-óz̃ù

Cold óyi
Cold dèyì
Cold íbù-óyi
Collapse žèé
Collapse ɔ̀ɗ̣ɗ̀à
Collect ná
Collect (water) chèrí
Comb ŋ̀shá
Come byá
Come by gàghásá
Come inside ɓànyísa
Come over gághàsá
Comedy ɔ̀kɔ́yị̀
Comic ɔ̀kɔ́yị̀
Common place nwàħí
Common Sense àkɔ́
Commotion gídígìdìgídí
Companion íbè
Comparison étù
Compassion ɔ́mìƙo
Compete m̃àtá-ókw̃ù
Competition ŋ́lebùtá
Complete mézù
Complete zùú
Completely kpám-kpám
Compound èzí
Comprehend ghɔ̀sá
Compress swàá
Conceal zwóħwòó
Conceal kpú kpùtɔ́
Conceive ṭùrɛ́-íme
Concerning gbásá
Concoct gwɔ̀ɔ́
Condition ɔ́nɔ̀dì
Conduct òmùmé
Conference ìkpù
Confidence óbù-íƙe
Confine tṵ̀-m̀kpɔ́rɔ́

Confinement m̀kpɔ́rɔ́
Confisicate jìcħyé
Confuse ghágwò jú ényà
Confused ị́gbà-m̃pa
Confused state ghárá-ghàrà-ghárá
Congeal kpṵ̀kɔ́tá
Congregate gbázwòó
Conjuctivitis ényá-ŋ́shi
Consider tṵ̀gháryá-úchè
Consider pàmàá
Conspiracy ìkpù
Contemplate chèé-échìchè
Contented person àmádi
Contract out làyí
Convene kpɔ́-òkù
Converse ħwṵ̀rí
Cook shí
Cook shìé
Cook shìtá
Cook wùú
Cook (till well done) ghèé
Coral beads kàláryà
Cord ṵ̀dɔ̀
Cork ókw̃úcħí
Corn ị̀kpákpà
Corn kernel ákpṵ́rṵ-ị̀kpákpà
Corner m̀ɒvákɔ̀
Corner ŋ́kɔ́
Corpse óžú
Corrode tàá-ṵ́járí
Corruption úre
Cost ɔ́nú-áfva
Costly óƙé-ɔ̀nu
Cotton wool ùrézè
Cough kwá

Cough ʉ́kwárà
Council ŋ́zùkɔ́
Counsel dw̃àá
Count g̃ʉ́
Count g̃ʉ́-ɖà
Count in (add) g̃ʉ́-nyi
Count out (subtract)
g̃ʉ́pʉ̀
Counter ɔg̃ʉ́ʉ̀
Country ógo
Court messenger kɔ́tùmá
Cover ókw̃ú
Cover kpú kpùtɔ́
Cover òkpú
Cover up kpùchȳé
Covet èzà
Cow éfĩ́
Cow námà
Cowardice àmʉ́mʉ̀
Cowry shell íkíríbyá
Crab ŋ̀kɔ́kɔ
Crab claws ɔ́kw̃áfá-ŋ̀kɔ́kɔ
Crack chìí
Crack chvé
Craft ŋ̀kà
Cramps ʉ́tá-ŋ̀gw̃ʉ̀fʉ̀
Cranny m̀pʋákɔ̀
Crave èzà
Crawl fĩ́
Crawl gbèé
Crawl ígbe
Crawl in ríɓà
Crawl off rípù
Crawl out rípʉ̀sá
Crawl up ríkʉ́fʉ́
Crayfish ɔ̀bʉ́ʉ̀

Crazy érá
Crazy person ónyé-fĩ́fĩ́fé
Cream mánú-òtíté
Create kèé
Creation ékìké
Creation òkị̀kè
Crewman kúrúmá
Cricket m̀bʉ́z̃ù
Cripple ŋ̀gwʉ́'fʉ̀
Criticize ŋ́kàkásị́
Crocodile áĝʉ́-íyi
Crooked gbèé
Crooked ḿgbéré
Crooked ŋ̀kɔ̀gbé
Cross òbé
Cross out kàgbwó
Cross over gbághàá
Cross over ŋ̃éghàá
Cross roads ègbàtà-úzɔ̀
Cross-eyed ényá-
ḿpághátá
Crosswise ùfúfȳè
Crown òkpú-ézè
Crush gbázwàá
Cry kw̃á
Cry ékw̃á
Cunning àkɔ́
Cup ìkó
Cure gwɔ̀ɔ́
Custom òméfálì
Customer ónyé-áfya
Cut wà
Cut bí
Cut gbùú
Cut ghèé
Cut z̃ʉ̀ʉ́

d

Dagger òpyó
Damp dèyì-dèyì
Damp ùdúdúru
Dance ťé-írí
Dance írí
Dancer óťè-írí
Dark óíi
Dark èťịlị̀
Dark of night àbàlísì
Darkness ìtìlì
Darkness ṇ̀íí
Dawn íshí-ákịká
Day chí
Day úbwɔchǐ
Day breaks bwɔɔ́ chí
Deaf-mute ìmúmù
Deafness ńchì-íK̃e
Death ɔ́nwú
Debt úgwɔ
Decaying úiárí
Deceive ghɔgbwó
Deceive mègháryá-ényà
Declare open mèpwó
Decomposition úre
Deep òmìmì
Deep ògbú
Defamation ṇ̀kàkásị́
Defeat mèrí
Defeat mèryé
Defile mèrwá
Deflate   h̃èé
Deliberate kèékè
Delight óbù-ụ̀twó
Demarcate kèwá

Denial ègị̃gó
Dent áru
Deny gɔɔ́
Departure ùlá
Depend upon chèmbé
Deposit kwụ̀wáyí
Depth ògbú
Design ègwà
Desire chɔ́
Destiny ákàrà-ɛ́kà
Destiny ụ̀wà
Destroy bíbyèé
Destroy làkásyá
Destroy mébì
Destroy mèkásyá
Destroy r̃ụ̀kásyá
Destruction ḿbíbí
Devil ékwénsu
Devouring òlúlwó
Dew íjí
Diabetes mámir̃ị-úkú
Diarrhea ĩe-ŋ́nɔ
Diarrhea ɔ̀nyụ́nyụ́
Die nwụ
Die (take a last breath)
ẑèé-úm̃ò
Die out nyụ̀h̃ụ́
Different íchò
Difficulty ịdị-íK̃íK̃é
Difficulty ḿkpà
Dig gùú
Dig into m̃àbaá
Dilapidated ḿgbéghéré
Dilate K̃ó

Dinner érímérí-àbàlì
Dip ɗòtú
Dirt ínvìr̃ì
Dirty rɔ̀tɔ̀
Dirty óyi
Discard tʉ́-ħwòó
Discomfort ghóró-ghòrò
Discomfort òghòròmà
Discover bw̃á
Discover chɔ́pʉsá
Disgrace mèchwó-íħw̃u
Disgrace mèkásyá
Dismantle làkásyá
Dismiss chwàá
Disorder gídígìdì
Disorder gídígìdìgídí
Disorderly ghághà
Disorderly ŋ̀lùghà-ŋ̀lùghà
Disorganize lásàá
Disorganize lɔ́sàá
Disputation ʉ́kà
Dissection ɔ̀bʉ̀bwɔ̀
Dissolve zèħí
Dissolve gbáryá
Dissolve gbáz̃èħí
Distant íbe
Distribute ʈúsàá
Ditch ɔ́bʉ̀
Dive into m̃àbaá
Divide kè
Divide wà
Divination ɛ̀ìà
Divine gbàá-ɛ̀ìà
Diviner ɔ̀gbá-éjà
Division òkè
Division ŋ́kèwá
Dizziness ɛ́nyá-éjʉ̀
Dizzy éjʉ̀

Do mé
Doctor díbyà
Dodge zèé
Dodge gbá-ʉ̀rĭghì
Dodge ħèé
Dodge ʉ̀rĭghĭ
Dog ŋ́kĭta
Doodle ɛ̀sátɔ-ńsèkátá
Door ʉ́zɔ̀
Door ígbàghàrì
Door frame íkwúghú
Double face íħw̃úr'àbwɔ̀
Doubt óbù-ɛ̀bwɔ́ɔ
Dragonfly ŋ̀dùm-ŋ́tà
Draughts èpèlé
Draw gwòó
Draw sé
Draw dɔ̀ɔ́
Dream rɔ̀ɔ́
Dream ŋ́rɔ́
Dredge chàá
Dress dùbá
Dress ŋ́wéyí
Dress up dʉ́rʉ̀
Dribble kpé
Dried corn ákáchĭ
Drill fyɔ́ɔ́
Drink ñùú
Drink ɔ̀ŋ́ʉ́ñú
Drink up ñùr̃ú
Drinking ɔ̀ŋ́ʉ́ŋ́ʉ́
Drinking party ɔ̀ŋ́ʉ́ŋ́ʉ́
Drinks mányí
Drip gʉ̀ʉ́
Drip ʈá
Drive ŋ́á
Drizzle kɒà-ḿbwɔ̀
Drop gbɔ̀tɔ́

Drums ìkpìrìkpè
Drumsticks ákwàtánkwà
Dry kpɔ́
Dry m̃í
Dry season ɔ́kɔ́chị̀
Dry up tàá
Duck úgbàlà
Dung ŋ̀shí

Dung beetle ádantà-ɔkpú-ńsh̃í
Dust úz̃ú
Dusty ŋ̀tụ́ŋ̀tụ̀
Dwelling òbúbú
Dysentery áyíghá
Dysmenorhea ók̃é-òshì

e

Each kwà
Eagle ùg̃ò
Ear ŋ́ch̃ì
Ear infection ŋ́ch̃ì-éɓù
Early èwà
Early morning ísí-ụ̀tụ́tụ̀
Earn r̃ụ̀sá
Ear-ring ífé-ŋ́ch̃ì
Earth élu-ụ̀wà
Earth worm ídìdè
Earthen-bed óji
Earthworm ìsìsìboloyi
East ɔwụ̀wá-ányánwu
Easy m̀fé
Eat ryé
Eat all rìgbwó
Eaves èh̃wụ̀rụ̀
Eczema úgwà
Edge out fípù
Eel ŋ̀ták̃i
Efficacious ìrè
Egg èkw̃á
Egg-plant áŋàr̃à
Eight èsátɔ

Eighteen ìrí-èsátɔ
Either mɔbụ̀
Elbow m̀pù-ékà
Elderly person ónyé-ìch̃ỹè
Electric fish èrùrù
Elephant ényí
Elephant grass égbé-ògùgù
Elephantiasis ɔ́kpà-ébì
Emaciate jɔ́-h̃wụ̀
Emerge pụ̀sá
Empty m̃kpɔ́kɔ́rɔ́
Empty ɔ́kpɔ́kɔ́rɔ́
Empty bottle ɔ́kpɔ́kɔ́rɔ́-ékpém
Empty sack ɔ́kpɔ́kɔ́rɔ́-èkpà
End swɔ́ɔ́
End ụ̀swɔtụ̀
End òbùbù
Endeavor m̃gbálị́
Ended óbùláa
Endless ágwụ-ágwụ

Endure gbàbá
Enema   òK̃èn
Enema ùkébè
Enfold ñ̃wùbá
English man bèkéè
Enough tùú̧
Enough zùú
Enough ñ̃àá
Enrich mèbá
Enter ɓànyí
Entirely kpám-kpám
Envious ényá-ú̧ñ̃wú
Epilepsy èkwú̧kwù̧
Equal ĩ̧ñ̃àtíñ̃à
Equal ñ̃àtá
Erase ñ̃wúpùú
Errand ózí
Escape gbàtáñ̃ú
Escort dùú
Eulogize twòó
Evening ɔ̀ɡb'ésì
Event èkwà
Everybody ɔ̀ñ̃à
Evil ĩ̃fé-ɔ́jɔ́ɔ
Evil jɔ̀njɔ

Evil ɔ́iɔ́ɔ
Exact kpɔ́m-kwèm
Exactly ényáya
Examine tù̧lé
Excess ĩ̧bàghàbú̧ghú̧
Exchange tú̧-nwòó
Excreta ŋ̀šhí
Exfoliate pó
Exhale m̃óɗà
Exhaustion íK̃é-ɔ̀ɡwú̧gwú̧
Exhortation ɔ́ɗu
Expensive óK̃é-ɔ̀nu
Expensive óK̃é-ɔ́nu
Expensive ɔ́nú–ikiK̃e
Extinguish ñ̃wú̧-nyú̧á
Extinguish mènyú
Extinguish nyù̧ñ̃ú̧
Extol ĩ̃ú
Extraordinary áñ̃ányí
Eye ball ḿkpú̧rɛnyà
Eye brow ìkù-ényà
Eye lashes ìkù-ényà
Eyeglasses ényá-bèkéè
Eyes ényá

f

Fabric éK̃ù
Face íñ̃wú
Face to face íñ̃wúr̂íñ̃wú
Fade chàbwɔ́
Fade chú
Faded nwàñ̃í
Faeces ŋ̀šhí

Failure ɔ̀ɗ̧ɗà
Failure kw̃á-ɔ́K̃ú
Faint ɗàá-m̀bà
Faintness m̀bà
Fake òfèK̃é
Fake àdígbòlója
Fall ɗàá

Fall ɔɗ̣ɗà
Fall ɛɗà
Fall sick žèé
Falsehood ḿgbàghátá
Falsehood ụ̀ghá
Falseness íɦw̃úr'àbwɔ
Fame ùɗé
Fancy òyóyò
Far ɛnyá
far off dì-ɛnyà
Far off ɛnyá-ènyà
Far place íbé-ɛnvà
Farewell íjè-ɔmá
Farm úbì
Farm basket ábwɔ
Farm settlement óɡo-úbì
Fart ɛ́ɦụ̀
Fashionable ŋ̀g̃àng̃à
Fat íbù
Fat èɓụ̀ɓà
Fate ákàrà-ɛkà
Father ŋ́nà
Father-inlaw ŋ́nà-ji
Fault ɔ́rụ́
Fear égw̃ù
Fearless átụ-égw̃ù
Fearless égw̃ù-átu
Feast òkù
Feather ɛbụ́bà
Feel around píkàá
Female àm̃ị̀
Female nwámì
Fence ɔ́kà
Festival m̀mèm̀mé
Fetch (water) chú
Fete m̀mèm̀mé
Fetish mánɡ
Fetish ɛ́r̃únsị̀

Fiery coal óbwókɔ́ʛu
Fifteen ìrí-ìšó
Fig ɔ́ɡbụ́
Fight ɔ́g̃ụ̀
Fight lụ́ụ́
Fight lwàá
Fighting ɔ́g̃ụ̀
Figure g̃ụ́
Filariasis ɔ́kpà-ébì
File ígbèghìrì
Fill gbàjwó
Fill up mèjú
Filter zàá
Find bw̃á
Find chɔ́sá
Find fault ʔàá-ụ̃̀ta
Fine ɔ́má
Finger ḿkpísị-ɛkà
Finish gwụ́
Fire ɔ́ʛú
Fire flies kúkúńdà
Fireside ɛnvár̃ɔ́ʛu
Firewood ŋ́ʛú
First m̀bụ́
First daughter àɗá
First son ɔ́kw̃ár̃á
First wife ŋ̀nékwú
Fish áz̃ù
Fishing hook ègwéyí
Fishing net ùɡbú
Fishing net ŋ̀tófo
Five ìšò
Fix mèzyé
Flatness m̀bádámbá
Flesh ánú-ɦwụ́
Flight ùfé
Flirtation ị̀kpɔ̀ghɔ́
Float sérélu

181

Flog lɔɔ́
Flood íɗònyí
Flood àbáráwóm
Flower òkó-òkó
Flower òkóryè-ɔ́cħá
Flu ímí-ómúmé
Flute ɔjà
Flute òpù
Fly fé
Flying termite ùkpɔmǐr̃ǐnkícħǐ
Foam ùtɔrɔħ̃wúħ̃wù
Follow ̃só
Follower ŋ̃s̃òghòr̃àʒ́ú
Followers ̀egbùrù
Food érímérí
Food ŋ́dí
Foot úkwú
Foot bridge àkw̃ùkw̃à
Foot path ùgárá
Foot steps ìkìtì-ɔ́kɒà
Footpath ̀eríí-úzɔ̀
Footsteps úkwú
Forceps m̀kpà
Foreigner ónyé-mbà
Forest m̀gbóko
Forest ɔ́kàyì

Forest ɔ́fyá
Forget rìzɔ́ɔ́
Forget zɔ́ɔ́
Forgiveness ̀ebérè
Forgiveness ̀egɔ́
Fork ŋ̀kɔ́m-éze
Forked wàá-ŋjàkɒà
Forty íħ̃wúr'àbwɔ̀
Four ̀enó
Four hundred ńnù
Fourteen ìrí-̀enɔ́
Fragment ḿkpìrìkpì
Frequency ŋ̀tú
Friend ényì
Frighten mèsí
Frighten mènyí-égw̃ù
Frog m̀bàrá
Front íħ̃wú
Froth ùtɔrɔ̀ħ̃wúħ̃wù
Fruit ḿkpúrù
Fruits ḿkpúrù-ósísí
Fry ghèé
Fulfil mèzwòó
Full jù
Fungi érwó
Funnel ágbúgbá
Funny ɔ̀kɔ́yǐ

g

Gall bladder ḿgbílu
Game ḿmérí
Gap-toothed éze-úzɔ̀
Garden úbi-ézi
Garden egg ùɓóghǐnǐ

Garment ŋ́wéyí
Gather tútwàá
Gather chìkátá
Gather nùr̃ú
Gather zúkɔ̀ɔ́

General ɔchí̜-ɔ̃g̃ù̜
Genuine ézíya
Germinate púpùsá
Germinate pú
Germinate pwó
Get lost gbáĥwùĥú
Get well ɗi̜ĥí
Ghost máng
Gigantic àg̃àgĥàr̃à
Gingivitis ámámfṽa
Girl nwá-àgbɔ́ghɔ̀
Girl nwágbɔghɔ̀
Give ní
Give injection šó-ɔ́gwù̜
Give way n'óhèrè
Give way n'éfè
Gizzard éƙò
Gizzard ábàchí
Glare nwú
Glare at nwú̜nwàsyá-ényà
Glass ènyò
Glue m̀gba
Glue onto nyànɗé
Glutton ókpómpí
Gnash tàá-íkìkére-éze
Gnash íkìkére-éze
Gnaw tàá
Go gàá
Go gàní
Go j̃èé
Go on gàĥé
Go on g̃é
Go out nyù̜ĥú̜
Go over gbágĥàá
Go with šó
Goad gbàyí
Goad jáɓàá
Goat éwú

god chí
God Chínekè
god ɔbàsi̜
Goitre ŋ̀kɔ́lɔ̀-ékpù̜
Gong ògélè
Good ézí
Good ḿma
Good ɔ́má
Good luck íĥwú-ɔ́má
Good person ézí-maɗu̜
Goodness óbù̜-ɔ́má
Goods ŋgwá-áfya
Goose pimples ékpi̜kpá-íbù̜-óyi
Gorge ágbɔ́-ókókó
Gorrila ɔ́zɔ̀
Gossip símsi̜msi̜m
Gourd àgbɔ̀
Governance ɔchí̜chí̜
Grab ɓá
Grab ɓànɗé
Grab fyé
Graceful ĩ̜jè-ág̃u
Grandfather ńnàńnà
Grandmother ŋ̀né̀ńné
Grass ìchíta
Grass éfífyá
Grass-cutter ŋ̀chì
Grasshoper chíchíchí
Grave ílì̜
Gray hair íshí-ɛ́wɔ
Gray hair ɛwɔ́
Great óƙé
Greater ɔkà
Greater kà
Greed óƙé-ɔchí̜chɔ́
Greedy ényá-éƙá
Greet kèlé

Greetings èkélè
Gregarious bwághá-bwághá
Grime èkpí
Grind gwòó
Grind kwó
Groan úɗè
Groan íkpɔ-ésè
Grooming ŋẓụ̀ẓụ̀
Groundnuts àn̄wékéré
Group òtù
Grow twòó
Grub ákpúghúrí
Grumble támù

Grunt s̄ụ́-úɗè
Grunt úɗè
Guard ché
Guarding òchíché
Guess work ákụ̀mákụ̀
Guinea fowl ɔgàzụ̀
Guinea worm étụ́ ékérè
Gully ògùgù
Gum m̀gba
Gum égbụ̀
Gun égbè
Gun-powder ŋshí-ègbè
Gut bwɔ́ɔ́
Gutter ɔ́lárá-mini

h

Haemorrhoids ùnùghùnúghù-ɔ̀kpụ̀
Hail t́ú-éfà
Hair éíí
Hair ègbísị̀
Half ŋ́tìkpìrì
Half portion m̀kpị̀
Half-penny áfù
Halfway ègbàtà
Halt gbòchwó
Hamstring ètè-ɔ́kpà
Hand éká
Hand made éká-mèrè
Hand-held fan àkùné
Handiwork éká-ɔ́r̃u
Hang nyàr̃í
Hang dùgbwó
Happen gbà

Happiness óbù-ụ̀twó
Hard ìk̃ík̃é
Hard-heartedness óbù-ŋk̃úmà
Harmattan úgụ̀rụ̀
Harvest ghɔ́rú
Haste ŋ́gwá
Hat òkpú
Hatred àsị̀
Hatred író
Haul tụ̀ụ́
Hawk égbé
He goat m̀kpí
Head íshí
Head ache ɔ̀wụ̀wá-íshí
Head tie ísí-ɔ̀k̃àr̃à
Head-ache ísí-ɔwụwa
Heal gwɔ̀ɔ́

Healthy ħwú-ítaħiǩe
Heap ítù
Hear nu
Heart ḿkpú̱robù
Heart óbù
Heart-burn ɔ̀nù̱nù̱
Hearth ékwũ
Heat rash ékị́rị̀-m̀bàħwũrũ
Heaven Àlị̀-ézé-Chínekè
Heaven élu-ígwo
Heaven ígwo
Heavy ígbíjí
Heavy laden nyìgbú
Heel ãτù-ɔ́kpà
Height éǩá
Hell ɔ́ǩú-àlị̀-ŋ́mɔng
Help yèé-ékà
Hepatitis ékɔ̀m-ényá-òɖò
Here ébáà
Hiccups étùtúru
Hide ákpú̱kp
Hide zwòó
Hide and seek òló
Hiding ŋ̀zù̱zwó
High èħwùrù
High fever óǩé-òyi
High jump ɔ̀tù̱rùkpɔ́
High noon òg̃èřé-òwù
High price óǩé-ɔ̀nu
Hill úgwú
Hillock ḿkpúŋkpú
Hippopotamus ényí-mini
Hire ŋ̃ù̱řú̱
History àǩá
Hobby ɔ́ǩù
Hoe ɔ́g̃ù̱
Hoe handle égbérè
Hold down ɓànɖé

Holds jì
Hole ókóghóró
Hole ŋ́túbe
Holiday m̀ɓúɓú
Holy ŋ́sɔ́
Honey mánú- éŋ̃u
Honour sɔ
Hope on chèrí
Horn m̀pù
Horn òpù
Hornet èbù
Horse ìnyìnyà
Hospital úlwò-ɔ̀gwu
Hot ɔ́ǩú
Hot body ħwú̱-ɔ́ǩu
Hot drinks mánvi-ɔ́ǩu
Hot tempered ŋ̀kị́rị́
Hot-tempered óbù-ɔ́ǩu
House úlwò
House flv ñ̃ii
How? ŋ̀dáà
Hug bỹe-ɔ́mà
Hug ìɓye-ɔmá
Human being máɖù
Human beings ŋ́dí-iře
Humiliate mèchwó-íħwũ
Hunch on back ḿkpúnkpú-àz̃ù
Hunger ɛ́g̃ú
Hunt chụ-ńtá
Hunter dínta
Hunting ŋ́tá
Hurry up gbàá-éká
Hurting ħwù̱ǫ́-ù̱ħwú̱
Husband íí
Husband ŋ́nà-úkú
Husk nwò
Hydrocele íbì

Hyprocrite íh̃w̃úrʾàbwɔ̀

i

Identification marks áh̃ùmá

Idiocy ŋ̀zúzù

Idiosyncrasv ékè

Idol éɾ̃únsị̀

Idol ùkɒátá

Idol éɾ̃únsị̀-áp̃ĩ̀r̃àp̃ĩ́

Ignorance ámàghị̀

Illiterate ìgbí

Ill-treat mègbú

Illustrate gwòó

Image éɾ̃únsị̀

Imitation àkpụ̀ràkpú

Immediately ꞌtà

Immortal ánw̃u-ánw̃u

Impassable chỹé

Important ɓà-úrù

Impound jìch̃yé

Imprison tụ̀-m̀kpɔ́rɔ́

Imprisonment m̀kpɔ́rɔ́

In é

Including èyé

Increase ụ̀bá

Indecision óbù-ὲbwɔ́ɔ

indigestion àtùkpú

Inform zyèé

Inhale m̃òɾ̃ú

Initiated ɓá

Injure mèió

Inlaw ɔ́gɔ̀

Inner room m̀kpúrù

Innoculation m̀kpòsúm

Inoculate šó-ɔ́gwụ̀

Inquiry èsè

Insanity ĩ́ĩ̃fé

Insert wàyí

Inside íme

Instead ƙámà

Instruct ží

Instruct ŋ̀ɗùmɔ̀ɗù

Intelligence ŋ́kɔ́

Inter páɓà

Intestinal worm áríɾí- ɛ́ƙá

Intestines ákị̀ɾị̀- ɛ́hwɔ

Intimidate mènyí-égw̃ù

Intoxicate pàá

Intrepid égw̃ù-átu

Intrepid átụ-égw̃ù

Invitation òkù

Iroko tree ɔ́j̃ì

Iron ígwò

Iron pot ìtè-ígwò

Iron sheet chán

iron-monger ɔ̀kpụ̀-ụ̀žụ̀

Is bù

Is dì

Itch ɔ́kɔ́

Jab ɗùú

Jab gùú

Jail tụ̀-m̀kpɔ́rɔ́

Jam dú

Jam swɔ̀ɔ́

Jaw àgbà
Jealous ɛ́nyá-ụ́ñwú
Jelly-like ròkóròkó
Jewelry ɔ́là
Jigger ŋ́dɔŋ
Joke èwụ̀
Journey ĩ́è
Journey ǹìèm
Joy ɔ́ñ̃ù
Judgment íkpe
Juicy ɔ̀sụ́kwụ
Juju ɔ́gw̃ù

Jump fé
Jump m̃á
Jump across m̃á'ghàá
Jump over m̃àfé
Junction ègbàtà
June beetle bèríbe
Jungle ɔ́kàvì
Jungle óƙé-ɔ́fva
Jungle ɔ́fyá
Junk élụ̀ghụ́lú
Just right tụ̀ụ́
Jute bag èkpá-ŋ̀vụ̀rụ̀mà

k

Keel over ŋ̃àbúkɔ́
Keep dèbé
Keep moving g̃é
Key ɔ́kpɔ́ghɔ́rɔ́
Kidnap kwùtáa
Kidney áƙị-ḿkpụ́ŋ́kpụ́
Kill gbwòó
Killer ògbúù
Kind óbù-ɔ́má
Kindle mètú
King ézè
Kingdom of God Àḷị-ézé-Chínekè
Kitchen ùs̃ókw̃u
Kitchen knife ḿmà-ékw̃u
Kite éɡbé
Kite ŋkwɔ́

Knead pị̃
Knead pìgháryá
Knee íkpèrè
Kneel bùsíbé
Knife ḿmà
Knock kụ́
Knock down kụ̀twó
Knocked knee íkpèré-ŋ̀kɔ̀gbé
Knocked-knee ɔ́kpà-ŋ́gbéré
Knot ékpụ̀
Know má
Know màrĩ́
Kola-nut ɔ́íí
Burn kpɔ̀-ɔ́ƙu

l

Lacking énwòghừ
Ladder úbùbé
Ladle m̀kpíkpá
Ladle ékú
Lamb ā̄túr̃u
Lame ŋ̀gwʉ́'r̃ʉ
Land àɲ̀
Land đàá
Language ásùsú
Language ókwú
Lantern òtéríkáng
Lap àpàtà
Large àyàwùrù
Large gbàghà-gbàghà
large number ŋ́nʉ̀
Large piece ókpʉ̀rʉ̀kpʉ̀
Large spoon ékú
Last year àk̃áh̃ì
Late ábyaghị-ŋ̄gwã́ŋgwã̀
Latrine úlwò-ŋ́nɔ
Laugh chʉ́í
Laughter óchʉ́
Law ìwú
Lax bèghè-bèghè
Laziness èg̃àr̃à
Lazy ùgèdú
Lead chʉ́
Lead astray r̃áh̃wùú
Leader ónyé-ísí
Leaf ékwʉ́kwɔ́
Learn mù
Learn mwàá
Leash ɔ́gbʉ́
Leather ákpʉ́kpɔ́
Leech étu

Left m̀bʉ́rʉ́
Left hand ɛ́ká-m̀bʉ́rʉ́
Left handed ɛ́ká-ʉ̀kpà
Leg úkwú
Leg ɔ́kpà
Lemon újíri-ɔ̀gw̃ʉ̀-ŋ́ma
lend (to someone)
gbàz̃ínyí
Leopard ág̃ʉ
Leprosy èkþèntá
Less ádịya
Levy ch̃òó
Liar írér̃'àbwɔ̀
Lid ókw̃ú
Lie ghàví
Lie ĵár̃i
Lie ʉ̀ghá
Lie ĵághàá
Life ŋ́đù
Lift off bùú-pù
Lift off (a cooking pot)
h̃wɔ̀pʉ̀
Lift up bùú-lyé
Lift up pàlyé
Light mùnyí
Light ìf̃è
Light up nwùr̃ú
Lightness m̀fé
Like ìlèghè
Like this ŋ̀ní
Lime újíri-ɛ́ghíríghá
Limp ĺé-ɔ́kpà
Lineage ègbʉ̀rʉ̀
Lion òdúm
Lion ɔ́dʉ̀m

Lips   ógbóro-ɔ́nu
Liquor glass   àkàràsị̀
Listen   ɛ̃èbé-ńcħì
Listen   ŋ̀àbá ŋ́cħì
Lively   bwághá-bwághá
Liver   íméịi
Lizard   ŋ̀gw̃ụ̀r̃ụ̀
Load   íbú
Loan   gbàžínyí
Lock   gbàchỹé
Locust   ìgùrùbè
Loitering   ŋ́tụrìí
Long   ɛ́k̃á
Long matchet   òg̃è
Look at   kálá
Loose   bèghè-bèghè
Loosen   tɔ́ɒùɥ́
Lorry   ụ́gbɔ́-ali

Lose   túħwòó
Lose weight   jɔ́-ħwụ̀
Loss   ħwùú
Loss   íbì
Loss   ʂ̃ùɥ́
Loss   ŋ́ʂ̃ù
Loss   ʂ̃ụ̀ɥ́- áfyá
lost   ħwòó
Lot   ìgbùdù
Louse   ígwú
Love   r̃ùú-ɛ́nvá
Love   ĩ̀r̃ur̃ènyá
Low groan   ʂ̃ɥ́-úɗè
Lukewarm (water)   rụ̀ká-rụ̀ká
Lumps   ɛ́kpɥ́kpú
Lure away   tụ̀rɥ́

m

Machete   ḿmà-òg̃è
Mad person   ónyé-ɛ́ra
Madness   ĩ̀r̃ĩ̀fé
Madness   ɛ́rá
Maggot   ìkpúrikpú
Magic   m̀màr̃ɔ́gw̃ụ̀
Maid   nwántà-ụ́žù
Maiden   nwágbɔghɔ̀
Maiden   àgbɔ́ghɔ̀
Main   ɔ́kw̃ár̃á
Main building   úlwò-ńtà
Main road   íħw̃ú-ụ́zɔ̀-ígwò
Main road   ókpóró-ụ́zɔ̀
Make dirty   mépàá

Malady   èlwà
Malarial fever   ɛ́kɔ̀m
Male   ók̃é
Male   ìk̃óm
Male   nwók̃è
Male lizard   ók̃e-ikpo
Malice   óbù-ɔ́jɔɔ
Man   nwók̃è
Man   nwókoro
Manifest   shí
Manilla   òkpòghò
Mannerism   ékè
Manners   ègwà
Manslaughter   ɔ́cħụ̀

Many ɔ́tú̧tú
Many ŋ́tú̧tu̧
Mark ókè
Market áfyá
Market price ɔ́nú-áfya
Marks èķíkà
Marry lú̧
Marry lù̧ú̧
Marry lwàá-ii
Marsh ɔ́rwá
Marvelous ébélébé
Mask ékpó
Masquerade ékᴅó
Masquerade ɔ̀kɔ́ŋkɔ̀
Massage nyù̧ú̧
Masses ɔ̀ñ̀à
Massive ógw̃ógw̃ó
Master ŋ́nà-úkú
Mat úté
Matches úrávíkáng
Matches ɔ̀kpá-sỹám
Mature twòrwòó
Me mwóo
Meandering túnkɔ̀rínkɔ̀
Meanness árúrú-àlì
Measles c̀ñ̀wù̧rì̧kpátá
Measure tù̧ú̧
Meat ánú
Medicine ɔ́gw̃ù
Medicine man díbyà
Meet ʈùtá
Meet kw̃ùnyí
Meet m̃àtá
Meet zúkɔ̀ɔ́
Meeting ŋ́zùkɔ́
Meeting ìzù
Melon ényú̧
Melon seed àñ̀wú̧

Melons élìlì
Melt gbáz̃èñí
Mend mèzyé
Mention (constantly)
ʈókpùú
Merchandise ŋ́gwá-áfya
Merchant ónyé-áfya
Mercy ḿgbáháŗ́
Merriment ñùŗ́
Merriment ŋ̀ù̧ryá
Message ózí
Metal container ògḇóŋ
Mid-air (Hanging)
èfètéfè
Middle èchìchì
Midnight èchíchì-àbàļì
Mightier ɔ̀kà
Mildew égbè-élígwó
Mildewed kw̃ù̧á-èbù
Milk míni-éɼá
Millipede és̃ú
Mimicry jíjè
Mimicry íjijè
Mirror ènyò
Mischief árúrú-àlì
Mischief ù̧rú̧
Mischievous ɼù̧ghérù̧
Miser éká-íƙe
Miserliness ákp̧ìkp̧ì
Miserly áñ̀ñ̀ì
misfire kw̃á-ɔ́ƙú
Misfortune iñ̀wú-ɔ́jɔ́ɔ
Mishap ɔ̀tá-mmàkwù̧
Mishap èghɔ́m
Mishap ɔ̀ghɔ́m
Mislead dúñ̀wùú
Miss kwàá
Miss nwáɖa

Miss lú
Mistake èghɔ́m
Mister mází
Mites ákpị̀
Mix gwàá
Mock jíjè
Mockery ɔ́chị́
Modern ɛ́lyá
Mold èbù
Mold kpụ̀
Mole ézìzì
Mollusk àkpàkóró
Money ìkpèghè
Money òkpòghò
Monitor lizared ághụ
Monkey ènwò
Month ɔ́nwá
Monthly salary úgwɔ-ɔ́nwa
Moon ɔ́nwá
Morning ụ̀tụ́tụ́
Morsel (of foofoo) ɔ̀kpụ̀
Morsel of foofoo ɔ̀kpụ̀-ụ̃̀tàr̃à
Mortar íkw̃ò
Mortgage íbe
Mosquito énwụ́ntà
Moth èrèkèrè-m̀búba
Moth ɛ́kw̃ụ́
Moth balls ɔ́gw̃ù-ɛ́kw̃u
Mother ìyáà

Mother m̀má
Mother ŋ̀né
Motorcycle kpèkpèkpè
Mould kpwàá
Mouldy kw̃ụ̀á-èbù
Mountain úgwú
Mourn kw̃á
Mourning m̀kpe
Moustache ɛ̃́íí-ímí
Mouth ɔ́nu
Move gàá
Move away nɔ̀láɦ́í
Move away nɔ̀pwó
Mow s̃wàá
Much ṹṍtṹ̃tu
Mud ùrùrɔ̀
Mud ɔ́rwá
Mumps àgbàńkpú
Munch tàá
Murder ɔ́cɦụ̀
Murderer òtbú-máɗù
Murmur támù
Mushroom érwó
Music írí
Musical instruments ŋ́kwà
Musk rat ɳ̀kákwu
Mutter támù
Myself mwóo
Myself ònwóm

n

Nail ḿbwɔ́
Naïve àjíjà

Nakedness ɔ̀tɔ́
Name gụ̀ụ́

Name ɛ́ɽà
Name sake ògbó
Nape ékw̃ù
Narrative úbùbwɔ̀
Narrow fyɔ́-ŋ̀fyɔ́ghɔ́rɔ́
Narrow wàrà-wàrà
Nation ḿbà
Native doctor díbyà
Naughty ílùghúlú
Nauseating dù̱ù̱-ɔ́nú-ɛ́gbɔ
Navel ótùbè
Nearness ŋ̀swó
Necessity ḿkpà
Neck ólú
Necklace ɽ̃ɛ́-ólù
Need ḿkpà
Needle àgìgá
Neighbour ɛ̀gbàtà
Neither mɔ̀bù̱
Nest ɛ̀kwú̱
New ɔ́h̃w̃úɽu
Newness ɔ́h̃w̃úɽu
Next year àʞá
Nice ḿma
Nice ɔ́má
Night àbàl̃ì
Night marauders àbàl̃ìdìmégw̃ù
Night vigil èzí-énvásì
Nimbleness ŋ́kɔ́

Nine tóolu
Nineteen ìrí-ètólu
Nipple ńnúnu̱-ɛ́ɽ̃a
No ɛ́ɛ̃-ɛ̀ɛ̃
No knowledge ámàghị̈
Noble àmádi
No-good òɽ̃èʞé
Noise ù̱žù̱
None-fitting áɓàghị̈
Nonsense ɽ̃ɛ́-èmúmà
Nook m̀pyákɔ̀
Nose ímí
Nose bleed òɓòghímì
Nostalgia ɛ́gwá
Nostrils ókóghóró-ímì
Novice ìtì
Now ʈà
Nubile girl nwá-àgbɔ́ghɔ̀
Nudity ɔ̀tɔ́
Nuisance ìgìrì
Number ɔ́nú̱-ɔ̃g̃u̱g̃u̱
Number ǹtú
Number ɔ́g̃u̱
Nursing mother nɔ́mɔghɔ̀
Nursing mother ŋ̀né-
ɔ̀mɔ́ghɔ̀
Nurture žwàá
Nut áʞị̈
Nut ákpú̱ru̱

O

Oar ɛ́dám
Oars ádám
Obese íbù

Obstacle ɔ́đàchì̈
Occasion èkwà
Occupation ɛ́ká-ɔ́ɽ̃u

Ocean   míní
Ocean   ènyı̌m
Off color   ákɒá-ı̌ɸè
Offend   mèjɔ́
Oil   mánú
Okra   ɔ́kwʊ̀rʊ̀
Old   óchỹè
Old age   ŋ́ka
Old man   ìch̃yok̃è
Old woman   ìchínyòm
Oldness   ŋ́ka
One   m̀bú
One   ŋ́ge
One   ólu
One hundred   íh̃wú-išo
Onions   àyúm
Only   ani
Ooze   nyʊ̀ʊ́
Open   sá
Open   tʊ̀pwó

Open   bwɔ́ɔ́
Open   gbàpwó
Open   kw̃ùpwó
Open   mèpwó
Open   sàpwó
Opening   óghere
Opportunity   óg̃è
Oppress   mègbú
Oppress   mènđé
Orange   újíri
Order   ʔʊ́
Outside   ákwà
Outside   èzí
Overcome   mèryé
Overtake   gbághàá
Overthere   íbé-ɔ́rı̌
Owl   ùkùghùkúghu
Own   nwò
Oysters   ákı̌rı̌syà

p

Pack   kwá
Pad   éjʊ́
Paddle   ɛ́dám
Paddle   ádám
Padlock   ɔ́kpɔ́ghɔ́rɔ́
Pain   úh̃wú
Pain   wùú
Paint   té
Paired   gbàà- ḿkpı̌
Palate   ókpólu
Palm (of the hand)   ɔ́bwɔ́-ɛ́kà

Palm fruit   ɛ́kwú
Palm Oil   mánú-ὲɡbʊ̀rʊ̀
Palm tree   ŋ́kwú
Palm wine   mányí-mini
Pants   ı̌bá
Paper   ɛ́kwʊ́kwɔ́
Parade   ʔó
Parcel   ŋ́gw̃ùɡw̃ù
Pare (trees)   gbɔ́ɔ́
Part   íbé
Partridge   ɔ̀kwà
Pass   gágha

Pass sá
Past year àfáñi
Patch nyàchỹé
Path úzɔ̀
Path ámã́
Path ùgá
Pathway òdwó
Patterns èkị́kà
Pawpaw ṁgbímgbí
Pay kwừá
Pay off mépừị́
Peace ùɗó
Peanuts àñwékéré
Peel ɓá
Peel ɓèé
Peep nyòó
Pellets àgìdì
Pen m̀kɒísị
People ŋ́dí-iﬁe
Pepper óšò
Peppery hot úñwú
Perch bèyí
Perfect énváva
Perfect kpɔ́m-kwèm
Perhaps íƙékwó
Periwinkles m̀fí
Perplexed gbàá-ṁpa
Perplexed ị́gbà-ṁpa
Perplexed ừtị́rừkátá
Person ónyé
Person máɗù
Perspiration éñw̃ị́r̃ừ
Pestle ɔ́ɗu
Phlegm ékpụkwàrà
Physician díbyà
Pick ghɔ́ɔ
Pick ñɔ̀rú
Pick (out) ñɔ́pừsá

Pidgeon kpálákuku
Piece íbéghéré
Piece ṁkpùghùrù
Piece ŋ́tìkpìrì
Pierce mã́
Pierce šùú
Pierce ɔ̀pwó
Pig éǯì
Pigeon ŋdùrú
Piggy-back kwɔ̀rị́-ɛ́wɔ̀
Pike m̀kpísị
Piles ùnùghùnúghù-ɔ̀kpừ
Pilfer ñèé
Pillow ǹché-ísí
Pilot ñá
Pin àgìgá
Pin worm èrúka
Pinch kɒí
Pipe ɔ̀kpɔ̀kɔ́
Pipe òɒù
Pipe ɔ̀ià
Pit ɔ́bừ
Pit ògùgù
Pit trap ɔ́bừ
Pity mé-èbérè
Pity ɔ́mìƙo
Place íbé
Place of sojourn úǯị́
Placenta élɔ́
Plait ƙèé-ĭsì
Plan m̀mừmà
Plant ƙú
Plant leaf m̀kɒé'kwụkwɔ
Plantain úkɔ́m
Plants áƙúmáƙú
Plate ừsàn
Play mèryé
Play ṁmérí

Play èwụ̀
Play ígburi-èwù
Plea árị̀ryɔ́
Please bíK̃o
Pleasure ùtwɔ́
Pleasure ŋ̃ụ̀rị́
Plentiful ụ̀bá
Plenty ìgbùdù
Plenty ìnùmàr̃à
Plenty ítùtù
Plenty ɔ́t̃ út̃ ụ́
Pluck ghɔ́rụ́
Plug up nyàchỹé
Plus èyé
Pocket èkpà
Point (with the finger) twàá
Poison ńshí
Polite ɔ́nụ-ɔma
Pomade mánú-òtíté
Pompous ɔ́K̃ómɔ́K̃ó
Poor person ógbèyì
Porch ŋ́kɔ́m̀gbè
Porcupine ébì
Pork ánú-éz̃ì
Portion òkè
Position (of authority) ɔ́kwá
Post òbé
Post ɔ́kwá
Pot ìtè
Potent ìrè
Potter ɔ̀kpúù
Pound sụ̀ú
Pounder ɔ́đụ
Pour wụ̀ụ́
Pour away wụ́h̃wòó
Pour in gbàyí

Poverty ógbèyì
Power íK̃é
Powerful ìK̃íK̃é
Praise twòó
Praise jàá
Pray íkperi-chi
Pray kpé
Prayer árị̀ryɔ́
Prayers èkpérè
Praying mantis ŋ́nàǹnam-ògbú-m̀pàm
Pregnancy íme
Pregnancy éh̃wɔ́-íme
Preparation ŋ́jiker̃e
Prepare mèbé
Prepare (soup) té
Present ní
Present day élyá
Press down bỹá
Pretty ɔ́má
Price ɔ́nu
Price ɔ́nu-áfyá
Price ɔ́nú-áfya
Prick đùú
Principal ɔ́kw̃ár̃á
Print bỹá
Probe đùú
Produce oil gbàá-mànù
Profession ɔ́K̃ù
Profit úrù
Promise ŋ́kw̃à
Prophecy ámụ́má
Prophesy bùú-ámúmá
Prosperity ùbá
Prosperity ɔ̀đĩ-ńma
Prostitute ɔ̀kpàrá
Protect chèbé
Protuberance ékpụ̀rụ̀kpụ̀

Proverb ílu
Provoke mènví-iwo
Proximity ŋ̀swó
Pubic area éɦé
Pubic hair éƙú
Public ɔ̀ɦà
Pull sèrí
Pull dɔ́ɔ́
Pull dɔ́
Pull nyàá
Pull sé
Pull down séɗà
Pull in séɓà
Pull out sépùsá
Punishment áfúfú
Pure ɔ́cɦà

Pure hearted óbù-úcɦa
Pursue chu
Pursuer ɔ̀chúù
Pus éɓú
Pus-filled ónwo
Push kwã́
Push nùú
Pussy cat nwám̀bá
Put yèé
Put dèbé
Put down gbɔ̀tɔ́
Put down méɗà
Put down (a load) žỹèé
Put in méɓà
Python éƙé

q

Quality ézí
Quarrel ùfyɔ́
Quarrel mètá
Quarrel ómétá
Quarrel ùžù
Queen ézè-nwami
Question ájùjú
Question èsè

Queue up šònyí
Quick ŋ́gwá
Quick and lively ğářá-ğářá
Quickly ŋ́gwá-ŋ̀gwà
Quietness ùdó
Quills éƙìƙà-ébì

r

Rabbit òkè-bèkèé
Rabbit ágálà
Rabies érá-ŋ́kíta
Race ɔ́sɔ́

Raches èkírị
Rafters ámímỹa
Rag ŋ́kághárị

Raggedly ŋkágháŕį-
ŋkagharį
Rain míní
Rainbow égwùgwù
Rainy Season ùdú-mini
Raise mèlyé
Raise up pàbúrú
Ram èbùlù
Rancid úka
Rash ékɒíkɒá
Rashes ɔ́kɔ́
Rat òké
Razor ágùbá
Reach rwòó
Reach rú
Read g̃ụ́
Read through g̃ụ́-ɗà
Reader ɔ̀g̃ụ́ụ̀
Real ézí
Real ézíya
Rear àʐú
Reason ìh̃í
Receive nàr̃í
Recognize màr̃í
Rectum ík̃è
Recur ŋ̀lụ́
Red ményi-ményi
Red úfyé
Red dye úfyé
Reddish úfúfye
Reflect tụ̀gháryá-úchè
Reflection àmụ̀mà
Refuge ɔ́sɔ́-ŋ́ɗù
Refuse gụ̀ụ́
Refuse jụ̀
Refuse dump úgwúr̃ír̃i
Reject h̃ụ̀ú
Rejoicing ɔ́ŋ̃ù

Relative íbè
Remain h̃wɔ̀ɔ́
Remainder úh̃wɔ́
Remember chèsá
Remember ŕįsá
Remove dúɒù
Remove lɔ́pù
Remove cover kpùpwó
Repair mèbézyé
Repair mèzyé
Repeat ŋ̀lụ́
Replace dèch̃ỹé
Reply sàá
Report úɗà
Report to zyèé
Reprimand ụ́ta
Reputation ùɗé
Request ár̃įryɔ́
Reserved ír̃ér̃e
Reside bù
Respect ùgw̃ù
Restless àghàrághà
Restlessness h̃wụ́-ɔ́k̃u
Retort sàá
Reveal kpùpwó
Revelation àmà
Revelation ŕŋkpùpwo
Revenge ífì
Revere sɔ
Revile kɔ́-ɔnu
Rheumatism ájú-óyi
Rhinoceros beetle
àkpàghàrà-íshí nkɔm
Ribs ákĭr̃i
Riches èk̃ụ̀
Ride gbàá
Ride ŋ̃á
Rifle égbè

Right hand ézí-ékà
Ring (a bell) kú̧
Ring nwɔ́là
Ring worm ákánkpɔ
Rinse tùsíɦá
Rinse ŋ́íŋ̀às̩íɦá
Rip làwàá
Ripen cɦá
Rising sun ɔwṳwá-
ányánwu
Rivalry ŋ́lebùtá
River míní
Road ú̧zɔ̀
Roam íɦo
Roast ɦw̃àá
Roast (corn) gbàá
Rock ŋ̀ƙúmà
Roll wòó
Roll around wòghátá
Room m̀kpúrù
Root ákw̃áɾ̃à
Root m̀gbàrɔ̀gw̃ù
Rope ṳdɔ̀
Rope érírí
Rot ré
Rot úre
Rotten teeth éze-órélá

Round gbùrùgbúrù
Round worm érírí-éƙá
Rub ɦwùú
Rub té
Rub tútwòó
Rubber ɔ̀kɒɔ́ɔ̀
Rudeness ɔ́nú̧-ɔ́jɔ́ɔ
Ruin bíbyèé
Ruin m̀bíbí
Ruin mébì
Ruin mèkásyá
Rule chí̧
Run (away) sɔ
Run away gbáɦwùɦú
Run away gbàtáɦú
Run away sɔ̀táɦí
Run by gbàghásá
Run into gbáɓà
Run into sɔ́ɓà
Run up gbàƙúɾ̃ú
Rust ŋ́káráfɔ́ng
Rust tàá-úiárí
Rust tàá-ŋ̀cɦaɾ̃a
Rust ŋ̀cɦaɾ̃a
Rusting (of metal or iron)
ú̧járí
Rusty tà-ŋ̀cɦaɾ̃a

S

Sac èkɒà
Sack èkɒá-ǹvṳrṳ̀mà
Sacred ŋ̀sɔ́
Sacrifice ƙú-éjà

Sacrifice èjà
Sail àfárà
Salary úgwɔ
Salt ŋ̀nú

Salute kèlé
Sand ɛ̃ja
Sandy clay ụ́tụ́-éfa
Sanitary inspector òlé-èfị́fyá
Sanity úɖò
Sap íkésu
Satan ékwénsu
Satisfactory jù-éɦ̃wɔ́
Sauce ófó
Sauce ỉ̃fé-ńdòrĩ
Saw ŋ̀kwɔ́
Say sị́
Scabbard ɔ́bwɔ́-ŋ́mà
Scald dá
scam ghɔ̀gbwó
Scar ḿpa
Scarcity ụ̀kɔ́
Scare ìɡìrì
Scare lábùsɔ́
Scare mènyí-égw̃ù
Scare mèsí
Scarf ákị̃sị̃
Scarf ísí-ɔ̃k̃àrĩ̀à
Scary dì-égw̃ù
Scatter gbásàá
School úlwò-ékwúkwɔ́
School child nwántà-úlwò-ékwúkwɔ́
Scissors m̀kpà
Scold ɖòsí
Scolding ḿbìgbɔ́
Scoop (into) ɦábà
scoop up nùr̃ú
Scorpion ákpị̃
Scorpion ákpị̃kpị̃
Scramble dwɔ̀ɔ́
Scrape kw̃ụ̀á

Scratch kɔ́
Scratch ɣ̃á
Scrawny (person) gédé
Scream chyé
Scribe ɔ̀gbá-ékwúkwɔ́
Scrotal sac èkpà-ámù
Scrotum ámù
Scrotum èkpà-ámu
Scrub ʃ̃á
Scrub tútwòó
Scrub zụ́zwàá
Scrutinize tụ̀lé
Sculpt kpwàá
Sculpt tụ̀ụ́
Scum èkpị́
Scurvy éwáká-ɔ́nu
Sea ènyĩ̀m
Seaport ɔ́nú-ésụ
Seat óché
Seat ɔ́nɔ̀dì
Seat àɣ̃àɖá
Seating ɔ́nɔ̀dì
Second World War ághá-Jámàn
Secretary ɔ̀gbá-ékwúkwɔ́
Section ḿkpị̃
See ɸ̃úú
See lèsá
Seed ákpụ́rụ
Seed ḿkpúrụ
Seek chɔ́
Seize kw̃ònyí
Seize jìcɦvé
Select ɦɔ́pụ̀sá
Self ònwó
Selfishness áɸ̃úɸ̃ú
Sell ré
Sell all règbwó

Send dùyí
Send down zìsá
Sensitive ézìzì
Sensitive (of teeth) gúgò
Separate íbú
Serve mènyí
Set shí
Set nyụ̀ụ́
Set (a trap) gbàbá
Set (fractured bones) gbàá-ɔ́kpụ́kpụ́
Set a fire vèé-ɔ̀kụ̀
Seven èsáà
Seventeen ìri-èsáa
Several ɔ̃ʃṹʃụ́
Severe ɔ̀nụ̀mà
Sew dw̃àá
Shabby púghú-pùghù-púghú
Shackles ókpórìmá
Shade ŋ̀dùrú
Shadow m̀bèm̀bè
Shake hands ná-ékà
Shaky ɦèghè-ɦèghè
Shaky tụ́tútú
Shame íɦéɾe
Shape kpwàá
Share kè
Share ʃú
Share òkè
Shark àtùmà
Sharp bone ógw̃u
Sharp sand ɛ̃ja-m̀bụ́rụ́
Sharpen m̃ú
Sharpness ŋ́kɔ́
Shatter wàá
Shave làá-íshì
Sheath ɔ́bwɔ́-ŋ́mà

Shed ɔ́đụ
Sheet ábáсɦá
Shell ókpòghóró
Shell ŋ́kìkére
Shield ɔ̃ʃtá
Shin íɦw̃ú-ɔ́kpà
Shine àmụ̀mà
Shine ké
Shine nwú
Ship ụ́gbɔ́-mini
Shoes ákpụ́kpɔ́-ɔ́kpà
Shoot gbàá
Shoot gbàgbwó
Shoot (of a plant) nụ́nụ̀
Shooter ɔ̀gbáà
Shop úlwò- áfyá
Short ḿkpụ́ŋkpú
Short ázà
Shorten swàá
Shorts ʃbá
Shoulders ŋ̀kùк̃úɾùbè
Shout chyé
Shout chyé-ḿkpú
Shout ḿkpú
Show ʒí
Show shí
Showy ŋ̀ǧàнǧà
Shrimps ópóró
Shrine íɦw̃ú-máng
Shrine ɔchúchú-èjà
Shrink from zèé
Shrubs ụ̀bwɔlɔ́
Shut mèchỹé
Shut eyes nyịsị́bá-énvà
Shut up mèchỹé-ɔ́nu
Shyness íɦéɾe
Sickness ùwàsi
Sickness èlwà**

Side ɛ́k̃ừk̃ừ
Sieve yàá
Sieve (dried grated cassava) gbáryá
Silent iàyì
Silk ŋ́k̃ị̀sị̃
Similar dìkàtà
Simply ɛ̀'m̀fé
Since íbé
Since ŋ́za
Sing g̃ṹ
Singer ɔ̀g̃ṹừ
Single ḿkpṹrừ
Sink mí
Sink mỹèé
Sit dùghá
Sit dùghá
Sit dùrú
Sit nɔ̀ghá
Sit kpɔ́g̃àr̃ị̃
Sixteen ìrí-ìs̃í
Sixty íh̃w̃ú-ɛtɔ
Skewer àgàjìrì
Skim off zàá
Skin ɛ́gbúgbɔ́
Skin ákpṹkpɔ́
Sky élu-ígwo
Sky ígwo
Slander ǹkàkás̃ị́
Slap lɔ́ɔ́-ékà
Slave óh̃wù
Sleep úr̃á
Sleep r̃àh̃í
Sleeping sickness úr̃á-ŋ́tà
Slice byé
Slide fvárárá
Slimy lɔ́ɔ́
Slip kwàá

Slip lú
Slot into fáɓà
Slow poke ùgèdú
Slugs m̀gbɔ
Small ŋ́tà
Small child nwántà
Smart àkɔ́
Smartness àmàmĩ́fé
Smash lɔ̀wàá
Smear té
Smell s̃hìé
Smell ís̃hi
Smell s̃hìé-ís̃h̃ì
Smell s̃hi
Smoke ɛ́nwừr̃ɔ́k̃ừ
Snail ŋ́jị̃lá
Snail shells íkìrìkè-ŋ́jị̃lá
Snake ágwɔ́
Snap jì
Snare ɔ́nyà
Sneak h̃èé
Sneak (away) h̃èĩáh̃í
Sneak (off) h̃épừú
Sneeze z̃í-ńdùghú
Snore gwɔ̀ɔ́-úr̃a
Snuff ɛ́nwừr̃ừ
So ŋ̀nó
Soak dèví
Soap ŋ́chà
Soft dèghèdèghè
Soft and mushy fàkàa
Soil mépàá
Sojourner nwá- ám̃úz̃ù
Sole (of the foot) ɔ́bwɔ̀-ɔ́kpà
Some ừfɔ́dị̃
Somebody ónyé
Somebody mádừ

201

Somersault ŋswɔ́-èbùlù
Something ĩ́fé
Something ífélèmantà
Son òkótà
Song έbụ̀
Soothsayer ɔ̀gbá-éjà
Sorcerv ḿ̩gbasi
Sore ɔ́nyá
Sorrowful ɔ̀nụ̀mà
Sound ụ́ɗà
Sound ɗàá
Soup ĩ́fé-ŋ́dòr̃i
Sourness (of soup gone bad)
ụ́ka
Space òpété
Space wà
Spawn àsímewɔ̀
Speak sụ̀ụ́
Speak kwú
Speak kpàyí
Spear árwà
Spectacles έnyá-bèkéè
Spend mén̄wú
Spendthrift έká-ɔ́k̃u
Spider ùɗíde
Spiders úkpị̃
Spill kw̃á-n̄wòó
Spill wụ́n̄wòó
Spirit máng
Spit out ɡbúɒụ̀
Split kpɔ̀wá
Split wà
Spoil mébì
Spoil mèkásyá
Sponge sàɒó
Spoon ŋ̀kɔ́m
Spotted twàá-ègwà
Spread gbásàá

Spread g̃èbé
Spring íyi
Sprinkle fé
Sprinkle ghàyí
Sprout pú
Spy nyòó
Squander (money)
tàkásyá
Squarter m̀byàràmbyá
Squash pyá
Squat túkw̃ùr̃ú
Squeeze fàá
Squeeze pị̃
squeeze into fàyị́
Squeeze into píɓà
Squeeze on pìnɗé
Squeeze out pípụ̀
Squirrel ɔ̃šá
Squirt nyụ̀ụ́
Stab m̃á
Stab šụ̀ụ́
Stab gùú
Staff m̀kpá
Staleness ɔ́rɔ̀
Stall ɔ́ɗụ
Stammering ŋ̀sụ̀
Stampcde gídígìɗìgídí
Stand gbàžụ́n̄ú
Stand g̃ụ̀žó
Stand (upright) g̃ụ̀žó-ɔ́tɔ
Stand up gbàžụ́n̄ú-ɔ́tɔ́
Stars kúkúŋ̀dà
Start mànyí
Start màlísá
Startle lábùsɔ́
Starve m̃í-έg̃u
State ɔ́nɔ̀dì
Statue ụ̀kpátá

Statue ɛ́r̃únsi
Stay nɔ̀ghá
Stay put nɔ̀nɗé
Steal kùtá
Steal ẓ̀ùrʉ́
Steal ẓwòó
Step aside nɔ̀ɒwó
Step on zɔ̀ɔ́
Stew ófó
Stick m̀kpaka
Stick óshíshí
Stick nyàá
Stick on nyànɗé
Stick to tàɼ́étɔ́
Sticky nyáɼ́ʉ́nyáɼ́ʉ́
Sting gbàá
Stink sh̃i
Stockfish ókpòròkò
Stoke sh̃òtú
Stomach ɛ́h̃wɔ́
Stomach-ache ɛ́h̃wɔ́-òbíbí
Stone ŋ̀ɼúmà
Stool óché
Stop gbòchwó
Stop gbòó
Stop mèchwó
Stopper ókwʉ̀ch̃í
Stopper (of a bottle or
gourd) ɔ́kwʉ́
Storey building úlwò-élu
Storm off (in anger) wàá-
ólìlyè
Storming m̀bìgbɔ́
Story ílu
Story ʉ́bʉ̀bwɔ̀
Stoutness ókpù
Stove ékw̃ú
Straight kpékpéré

Straight ɔ́tɔ́
Stranger ónyé-mbà
Stranger m̀byàràmbyá
Strangle pìgbwó
Straw ámì
Streaks ɛ́gɔ́rɔ́má
Stream íyi
Stream ògbèlé
Stream ŋ̀gèlé
Strength úm̃ó
Strength íɼé
Stretch sé
Stretch marks ɔ̀mùmú
Strike kpàyí
String érírí
String ŋ̃é
String (across) ŋ̃èchỹé
String beans kɔ́kɔ́nì
Stroke èkpèbɔ́ng
Strong ìɼíɼé
Strong dislike àsʉ̃̀
Struggle lʉ́kàá
Stubborn óbù-íkpútú
Stubborn íshí-ikiɼe
Stubborn nyàá-ísi
Stubborn ísí-ɔ́íɔ́ɔ̀
Stuck kwʉ̀tɔ́
Stuck gbàá-m̀pa
Study mwàá-ékwʉ́kwɔ́
Stuff into fàyʉ́
Stumbling block ɔ́ɗàch̃ì
Stump m̀kpìrìkpì
Stumped gbàkwʉ́r̃ʉ́
Stunted ázà
Stupid ìbèríbè
Stupid person ánù-mànù
Stupidity ŋ̀zúzù
Stupidity ìzúmá

Stupidly kpɔ̀sìí
Stuttering ɲ̀sụ̀
Sty ényá-ŋ́kíta
Submerge míɓà
Successor ṅ̄s̃òghòr̃àz̃ú
Succulent ɔ̀sụ́kwụ
Suck mỹàá
Suck mị́
Suddenness m̀bèrèg̃éɗé
Suffer ĩ́fusi-ènyá
Suffer táf̃ụ́f̃ụ́
Suffer tá-áf̃úf̃ú
Suffering áf̃úf̃ú
Sum ɔ́g̃ụ
Sum ɔ́nụ́-ɔg̃uẽ̀ụ
Summon kpɔ̀tụ́
Sun ánw̃u
Sunday ị́kɔ̀bàsì
Support chèrí
Surety íbe
Surety ónyé-ɛ́ká-ébe

Surface élu
Surpass kà
Surprise jù-ényá
Surround gbàgbùrù-gbúrù
Swallowing òlúlwó
Swallows èbántà-élígwo
Swamp ɔ̀gwà
Swamp ɔ́cha
Swear ŋ̀ụ̀àá-mang
Sweat éh̃w̃ụ́r̃ụ̀
Sweep zàá
Sweet níŋí-níŋí
Sweetness ụ̀twɔ́
Sweet-tasting ɔ̀twɔ́-níŋí-níŋí
Swell k̃ó
Swell (of welt) zàá
Swelling ék̃ɒùrùkɒụ̀
Swiftness ŋ́gwá
Swim gwú

t

Table ókpókóró
Tadpole m̀gb̲ìríwò
Tail ǹk̃ám
Tail ɔ́dụ
Tail ɔ́dụ̀dụ̀
Take nàr̃í
Take gwòrú
Take (a picture) gwòó
Take (all) gwòrúch̃ágbwó
Take (away) gwópù
Take a bath wụ̀á-h̃wú

Tale úbụ̀bwɔ̀
Talisman ék̃ík̃é
Talk úkà
Talk kpàyí
Tall ɛ́k̃á
Tap kpámòtú
Tarnish chú
Task ɔ́r̃ụ́
Taste ràtú
Tasteless sùsùrụ̀
Tasty ụ̀twɔ́

Tattered ŋ́kágháŕį́
Tattoo ìchi
Teach ʒí
Teach mù
Tear dɔ́-kàá
Tear ʃàká
Tear off ʃàr̃í
Tears ɛ́nyá-míní-ɛkw̃á
Teeth éze
Tell sį́
Tell kpàyírí
Tell (a story) ȟwų̀ų́
Temptation ɔ̀nwų̀nwà
Ten ìrí
Tendon ákw̃ár̃a
Termination òbùbù
Termination òchȟíchȟí
Termites àkų̀
Termites ɛ̀kį́kà
Testicles ḿkpų́rų-amų̀
Tete-a-tete ìkpù
That ɔ́r̃į̀
That (one) ɔ̀ȟų̀
Thatch ékį́r̃į́ká
Thatch roof ùȟúȟùr̃ú-úlwò
Theft óʃhí
Their wá
Them wá
There íbé-ɔ́r̃į̀
Therefore yà-me
Thigh àpàtà
Thing ĩ́ȟé
Things ŋ́gwóŋgwó
Think chèé
Think r̃į́
Think over r̃į̀ȟų́r̃ų́
Thinking ɔ̀r̃į̀r̃į̀

Thirteen ìrí-ètɔ́
Thirty óȟwú-là-ìrí
This ǹk'á
This ɔ́nwà
This à as in: ĩ́ȟéà (this thing).
This one ǹk'á
This way ŋ̀gw̃áà
This year áȟw̃àá
This year áfàá
Thorn ógw̃u
Thoughfulness ɔ̀r̃į̀r̃į̀
Thought échìchè
Thought úchè
Thread érírí
Thread gàyí
Threat m̀ɓá
Three ètɔ́
Threshold m̀gbè
Threshold ógbósígbó
Throat ŋ̀kɔ́lɔ̀
Throbbing gbéŋ-gbéŋ
Throne óché-ézè
Throw lɔ́ɔ́
Throw tų̀ų́
Throw away túȟwòó
Thump ĺị́
Thump lyàá
Thunder áḿų́m̃á
Tick ɛ̀kà
Tickle ɛ̀pų́rèpų́
Tie ȟé
Tie kw̃á
Tie lìbé
Tie on m̃àbá
Tiger fish ɔ̀kpɔ́
Tightness fá
Till tùtù

Tilt   ŋàá
Tilt around   ŋíŋàá
Time   m̀gbè
Time   óg̃è
Time span   óg̃è
Tin   cháŋ
Tin   ògbón
Tiny   ímúr̃ímú
Tip   núghǜnǜghú
Tip   núnǜ
Tip   ŋnúnṵ
Tiredness   íƙé-ɔ̀gwṵgwṵ
Toad   éwɔ̀
Tobacco   àsíkɔ̀n
Tobacco   énwǜr̃ṵ ,
Tobacco leaves   ékwúkwɔ́-énwǜr̃ṵ
Today   ʈààni
Toes   m̀kɒísị-ɔ́kpà
Toilet   ŋnɔ
Tolerate   rèbé
Tomorrow   échí
Tongue   íré
Tonsilitis   m̀gbápyá-ŋkɔ́lɔ̀
Tooth   éze
Toothache   ámámfỹa
Tooth-ache   éze-òmùmé
Top   ékésù
Top   élu
Topmost   núghǜnǜghú
Topple over   làbúkɔ́
Torch   yèé-ɔ̀ƙṵ
Tortoise   m̀bè
Total   ɔ́nṵ́-ɔg̃ṵg̃ṵ
Touch   bìtú
Touch   mètú
Tough   ɔ́kpɔ́nwúr̃ṵ́
Towel   ékwàmini

Town   óg̃o
Track road   èrírí-ṵ́zɔ̀
Trade zùú- áfyá
Trader   ónyé-áfya
Trader ónyé- áfvá
Tradition   òmér̃álì
Train   z̃wàá
Training   ŋ̀z̃ṵ̀z̃ṵ̀
Trample (to death)
zɔ̀gbwó
Transformation
m̀gbanwò
Transplant   dwɔ̀yị́
Trap   ɔ́nyà
Trash   éfífyá
Trash   élṵ̀ghṵ́lú
Trash container   ífé-éfífyá
Travel   ǹièm
Tray   ɔ́kwá
Tree   óshíshí
Tree stump   m̀kpó
Trench   ògùgù
Trial   ɔ̀nwṵ̀nwà
Tribal marks   ázà
Tribe   m̀bà
Trick   ghɔ̀ɔ́
Trickercy   ághṵ̀ghɔ̀
Trim   ɒé
Trip   ŋ̀jèm
Trouble   ìgìrì
Trouble   ùná
Trouble   ŋ̀ƙùkò
Troublesome   ǹƙùkò
Troublesome   ŋ̀níná
Troublesome (person)
àghàrághà.
Troublesome   àfàríkɔ̀ŋ
Trousers   ị̈bá

Trucks ụ́gbɔ́-ali
True ézí-ụ́kà
Truth ézí-ụ́kà
Try gbályá
Try out tụ̀tụ́
Tse-tse fly óso
Tuberculosis ụ́kwárà-ŋ́tà
Turn tụ̀gháryá
Turn ghá
Turn around gbàgháryá
Turn around ghàgháryá

Turn off (lamp or light)
gbànywá
Turn over tụ̀gháryá
Turtle ḿbè-míní
Twelve ìrí-èbwɔ́ɔ
Twenty óħwú
Twins èjìmá
Twist ghá-ụ̀bị̀bàrí
Twisted gbéghàtá
Two èbwɔ́ɔ
Tyrannize mènɗé

u

Ugliness ńjó
Ugly iɔ̀njɔ
Ugly ɔ̀bịlà
Ulcerating sore ágbú
Umbrella ŋ̀ché-ánwú
Unamenable ísí-ɔ́jɔ́ɔ̀
Uncover kɒùpwó
Undefiled ɔ́cħá
Under òkpúrù
Underestimate lèlyá
Underpart òkpúrù
Understand ɗòó-énvà
Understand ghɔ̀sá
Undress dụ́pụ̀
Unfailingly ághàghị̀
Universe ụ̀wà
Unkempt ŋ̀lụ̀ghà-ŋ́lụ̀ghà
Unknown ámàghị̃
Unmarried man ók̃é-
òkpòrò

Unripe ìkètá
Unripe ákaghaka
Untie tɔ
Until tùtù
Unwrap tɔ
Up élu
Uprightness ɔ́tɔ́
Uproar ḿbìgbɔ́
Uproar ụ̀z̃ụ̀
Uproot bụ̀rụ́
Uproot bùú
Urine mámị̃rị̃
Urn ètèrèkísɔng
Us ányí
Useless ḿkɒɔ́kɔ́rɔ́
Useless ĩfé-èmúmà
Useless ábàghị̃-úrù
Usurp nɔchṽé
Uterus èkpà-nwa

V

Valley ágbɔ́-ókókó
Van úgbɔ́-ali
Vegetable leaves úgbɔ̀ghɔ̀
Vehicle úgbɔ́
Venereal disease ŋ́shí-nwámì
Verandah ŋ́kɔ́m̀gbè
Vernacular ákpá-àlì
Vertical ɔ́tɔ́
Vessel úgbɔ́
Village óg̃o

Viper ɛ́ɓú-àlì
Visible bwɔ́.
Vision m̀ɍú
Visit ɛ̀bỹanyi
Visitor ónvé-ɛ́bỹanyì
Vomit gbɔ́ɔ́
Vomit ɛ́gbɔ
Voyeur ílùghúlú
Vulgar ílùghúlú
Vulture ùdèlè

W

Wage war bùú-ághá
Wager m̃àɍí-ɛ́kà
Wages úgwɔ
Waist úkw̃ù
Wait chètú
Waiting òchíché
Wake mɛ̆ɍé
Wake up ɩ̀èɍí
Walk ɩ̃ɩ̀è
Wall ɛ̀bịbàrà
Wall-gecko nwá-ŋché-úlwɔ̀
Wandering úɍị
Want chɔ́
Want ùkɔ́
Want ɛ̀zà
War ɔ̀g̃ù

War ághá
War dance ìkpìrìkpé-ɔ̀g̃ù
War dance írí-ághá
War leader ɔ̀chị́-ɔ̀g̃ù
Warn dɔ́ɔ́-ɛká-ńcɍ̃ì
Warning ɔ́đụ
Wash kwɔ́
Wash ꭍá
Wash (clothes) swàá
Wasp ɛ̀bù
Waste íbì
Waste méɍ̃wú
Watch lèbé
Water míní
Water leaf mányí-mányíkɔ̀
Water yam m̀bịlà

Wave vigorously fífỹe
Way úzɔ̀
We ányí
Weakness àmụ́mụ̀
Wealth òkpòghò
Wealth ùbá
Wealth èƙụ̀
Wealthy person àmádi
Weapons ŋgwá-ághá
Wear nyàá
Weave kpàá
Wedge fìví
Weed bwɔ́ɔ́
Weed (a farm) r̃ú
Weeding ír̃u-éfífyá
Weeds éfífyá
Weighty nyị́ị́gbĩ́jí
Welcome náɓàsá
Wharf ɔ́nú-ésu
What? ŋ̀gínị
When m̀gbè
Whetting stone ɔ̀m̃ùm̃ú
Which? òlé
Whimper íkpɔ-ésè
Whip ákánchu
Whip fỹèé
Whisper tákàví
Whistle ùkpɔ̀rɔ̀fífì
Whistle fvɔ́rɔ́rɔ́
White ɔ́cħá
White (cloth) ábácħá
White man m̀bàkárá
White man bèkéè
Whiteness ùcħá
Whitlow ágwɔ́-mang
Whooping cough úkwárà-ŋ̀kélu
Wickedness árúrú-àlì

Wickedness óbù-ɔ́jɔ́ɔ
Wickedness ùrú
Wickedness ńjó
Wide àbàdábà
Wide ɔ̀sịsá
Width m̀bádámbá
Width àbàdábà
Wild cocoyam òkóró-òkoro
Wild vegetable ụ́gbɔ̀ghɔ̀-ùrù
Wilderness ég̃u
Willingness úħére
Win mèryé
Win mèrí
Win (a trophy) rìsá
Wind ùfùfé
Winding túnkɔ̀rínkɔ̀
Window m̀gbúpwó
Window frame íkwúg̲hú
Windpipe ámi-nkɔ́lɔ̀
Wings ŋ̀kù
Wipe fỹé
Wisdom àmàmĩ́fé
Witchcraft m̃gbasi
Wither kpɔ̀nw̃úá
Witness ónyé-éká-ébe
Witness éká-ébe
Witty ɔ́rɔ́tɔ́ghɔ́-ụ́kà
Wobbly ħèghè-ħèghè
Woman nwámì
Woman ńchí-èkwà
Womb èkpà-nwa
Wonder èbùbè
Wonderful áħányí
Wood ŋƙú
Wood shelving ùkɔ́ƙu
Wooden bowl ɔ́kwá-ós̃ò

Wooden cymbals ájà
Wooden gong ékwó
Wooden platter ɔ́kwá
Woodpecker ɔ̀tʉ̀rʉ̀kpɔ́kpɔ́
Word ókwú
Work ɔ́r̃ú
Work r̃ú
Work r̃wàá
World ʉ̀wà
Worship kpé
Wound áru
Wrap gw̃ùú

Wrap up ƙèchyé
Wrapper cloth ɔ̀ƙàr̃à
Wrestling m̀gbá̱
Wrestling music ékwó-
ŋgba
Wrist ɛ́ká
Wrist-watch átáŋ-ɛ́kà
Write gbàá
Write gbàtú
Write gbàyí
Writer ɔ̀gbá-ɛ́kwʉ́kwɔ́
Wrong mèjɔ́

X

Xylophone ògúmògú

Y

Yam ŋ́dí
Yam barn ɔ́ɓa
Yam mound ókw̃ù
Yam seedlings ʉ̀kpírìkpɔ̀
Yawn ghɛ̀ɛ́-úghere
Yawn úghere
Year édʉ́-ìsì
Year áfà
Yearn for g̃ʉ̀
Yell ɓé
Yell ƙá
Yellow òɗò
Yellow fever ɛ́kɔ̀m-ényá-
òɗò
Yellowish òɗóɗò

Yes ívà
Yes ɛ́ɛ̃
Yes ãá
Yesterday ʉ̀nyàr̃i
You únù
Young man àkpàráwà
Young man òkóró
Young man òkóró-ɔ̀byà
Young woman nwáɗa
Yourself ònwóghu
Youth nwókoro
Youth òkóró-ɔ̀byà
Youth òkóró

Z

Zeal úñére
Zinc cháŋ